THE BIG LEAP

THE
BIG LEAP

Conquer Your Hidden Fear and

Take Life to the Next Level

GAY HENDRICKS, PH.D.

HarperOne
An Imprint of HarperCollinsPublishers

HarperOne

HarperCollins books may be purchased for educational, business, or sales promotional use. For information please write: Special Markets Department, HarperCollins Publishers, 10 East 53rd Street, New York, NY 10022.

HarperCollins Web site: http://www.harpercollins.com

HarperCollins®, 📖 ®, and HarperOne™ are
trademarks of HarperCollins Publishers

FIRST EDITION

Designed by Level C

Library of Congress Cataloging-in-Publication Data
Hendricks, Gay.
The big leap : conquer your hidden fear and take life to the next level /
Gay Hendricks.—1st ed.
p. cm.
ISBN 978–0–06–173534–9
1. Successful people. 2. Success in business. 3. Success. I. Title.
BF637.S8.H386   2009
158.1—dc22
2008051779

09 10 11 12 13 RRD(H) 10 9 8 7 6 5 4 3 2 1

Contents

Contents

THE BIG LEAP

Remove Your Last Obstacle to Ultimate Success in Wealth, Work, and Love

THE ONE PROBLEM THAT HOLDS YOU BACK

I call it the *Upper Limit Problem*, and I haven't met a person yet who didn't suffer at least a little bit from it. Even if you're already extravagantly successful, I can promise you that your own version of the Upper Limit Problem is still holding you back from achieving your true potential. In fact, the more successful you get, the more urgent it becomes to identify and overcome your Upper Limit Problem. If you don't clear the Upper Limit Problem out of your way, it will be a drag on you until the day you die. I know those words may sound blunt, but if our positions were reversed, I'd want you to be just that blunt with me.

I've taken the risk of speaking that bluntly to many people who were already quite successful. I did so not because they were paying me a consulting fee, but because it is part of my life's mission to help people go the last distance to claim their full potential. Michael Dell, founder of Dell Computer and one of the youngest self-made billionaires in history, is among the most brilliant people I've ever met. I had the pleasure of doing executive coaching with him and other members of his team during the nineties, at a time when the company was beginning to grow by leaps and bounds. The quality I most appreciate about Michael is his openness to learning. Many high-level executives I've known are saddled with an equally high degree of defensiveness and a deep need to be right all the time. Not Michael. He doesn't put on the brakes when new learning is coming at him. He doesn't have the tendency, shared by many CEOs, to resist change and do more of what obviously isn't working.

Michael embraces every opportunity to grow, and his remarkable success is testimony to the power of that point of view. That's the kind of openness to learning I'd like you to bring to our explorations together in this book.

Michael Dell wasn't born with his gift. None of us is. To get to that level of undefended openness to learning, we have to practice as diligently as a master skier or a master cellist. To make the kind of leaps Michael Dell makes, we must practice a specific skill. That skill is to identify and transcend our Upper Limit, wherever and whenever we encounter it.

We will hone this skill ceaselessly throughout the book. As Michael and others now know, the Upper Limit Problem is the only problem we need to solve. They dedicated themselves to solving it and made the Big Leap. The results speak for themselves.

Along the path to the Zone of Genius, all of them learned the same life-changing secret you will learn in this book: the glass ceiling they were operating under is held in place by a *single* problem—a barrier they didn't know they had. Once they saw the one problem—and how to solve it—they were free to go beyond ordinary success to a new and extraordinary level of abundance, love, and creativity in their lives.

Once you understand the one problem and how to solve it, you can do far more than increase your net financial worth: you can make quantum shifts in the amount of love you feel and the amount of creativity you express. I mention this point because I've learned that it is essential to keep the heart-and-soul elements of life—such as love and creativity—growing in balance as you go to higher levels of material success. It makes no sense to take your Big Leap into greater financial success in such a way that it destroys your relationships, your inner sense of yourself, and your connection to your inner wellspring of creativity. Many people have made that error, and the result is never pleasant to behold. Life is at its best when love, money, and creativity are growing in harmony.

In this book I want to talk to you directly, just as if you were sitting across from me, one-on-one. I may not know you personally, but based on my years of consulting, I believe I know a great deal about you. I imagine that you sense a huge unrealized potential in yourself, an extraordinary level of success you know you can achieve. I also imagine that you worry about falling short of achieving the ultimate success you can see, taste, and smell. If you feel that way, you're on the threshold of perhaps the greatest opportunity of your life. You're about to make a discovery that will remove the barrier between you and your ultimate success. I can make that promise to you because long before I helped other people enhance their own abundance, love, and creativity, I was my own best customer. From the moment of discovery until now, I have used the method I describe in this book to make all my own wishes and dreams come true.

THE MOMENT OF DISCOVERY

My original discovery happened early in my career, when I was working as a research psychologist at Stanford University. It was the moment I caught the first glimmer of the realization that would change my life so profoundly. Here's what happened:

I had just returned to my office from lunch with a friend, and we'd spent a congenial hour talking about the projects we were working on. My work was going well, and I was happy in my relationships. I leaned back in my chair and gave myself a good stretch, letting out a sigh of relaxed satisfaction. I felt great. A few seconds later, though, I found myself worrying about my daughter, Amanda, who was away from home on a summer program she had very much wanted to attend. A slide show of painful images flickered through my mind: Amanda sitting alone in a dorm room, Amanda feeling lonely and miserable away from home, Amanda being taunted by other kids. The inner joy disappeared from my body as my mind continued to produce this stream of images. Thinking something might be wrong, I grabbed the phone and called the dorm where she was staying. Her dorm supervisor told me Amanda was fine; in fact, she could see out the window to where Amanda was playing soccer with some other girls. The kindly supervisor told me it was normal for parents to worry about kids away from home; indeed, she said I was the third parent to call that day with similar concerns. "Really?" I said, surprised. "Why do you think that is?" She gave a wise chuckle: "You don't realize how much *you* miss *her*, so you think *she* must be hurting somehow. Plus, you probably had experiences yourself of being lonely away from home, so you think she must be having the same experience."

I thanked her and hung up. I felt a bit foolish, but I also knew that something important had just happened. I sat there wondering, "How did I go from feeling good in one moment to manufacturing a stream of painful images in the next?" Suddenly the light of awareness dawned on me: I manufactured the stream of painful images *because* I was feeling good! Some part of me was afraid of enjoying positive energy for any extended period of time. When I reached my Upper Limit of how much positive feeling I could handle, I created a series of unpleasant thoughts to deflate me. The thoughts I manufactured were guaranteed to make me return to a state I was more familiar with: not feeling so good. Worrying about children away from home is always a handy way to feel bad, but I knew that if I hadn't pulled up those particular worry-thoughts, I would have used some other train of thought to dampen my mood.

I remember almost dancing with excitement as I applied this insight to different parts of my life such as relationships and health. Once I saw the pattern, it became obvious how it worked: I would enjoy a period of relationship harmony, then stop the flow of connection by criticizing or starting an argument. The Upper Limit Problem showed up even in my eating habits: I would eat healthy food and get plenty of exercise, feeling great for several days in a row. Then I'd go on a weekend binge of restaurant food, wine, and late nights that would leave me feeling dull and bloated. The pattern was simple: enjoy a period of feeling really good; then do something to mess it up. I also realized that the same pattern had a grip on the world at large. As humans, we would enjoy a period of peace, then plunge into a war; we'd create a time of economic expansion, then go into recession or depression. Everywhere I looked, I saw evidence of the pattern. Eventually I reined in the wild horses of my imagination and focused on the key step every researcher begins with: stating the problem to be solved and the questions to be answered.

The problem:

I have a limited tolerance for feeling good. When I hit my Upper Limit, I manufacture thoughts that make me feel bad. The problem is bigger than just my internal feelings, though: I seem to have a limited tolerance for my life going well in general. When I hit my Upper Limit, I do something that stops my positive forward trajectory. I get into a conflict with my ex-wife, get into a money bind, or do something else that brings me back down within the bounds of my limited tolerance.

The problem looked much bigger than my own small version of it. Our species in general had grown accustomed to pain and adversity through millennia of struggle. We knew how to feel bad. We had millions of nerve connections devoted to registering pain, and we had a huge expanse of territory in the center of our bodies dedicated to feeling fear. Certainly we had pleasure points in various places, too, but where were the mechanisms for ongoing, natural good feeling? I realized that we were only recently evolving the ability to let ourselves feel good and have things go well for any significant period of time.

The first question I wanted to answer was this:

How can I extend the periods of contentment in my life?

Even better questions sprang up:

If I can eliminate the behaviors that stop the flow of positive energy, can I learn how to feel great all the time?

Can I allow things to go well in my life all the time? In relationships, can I live in harmony and intimacy all the time?

Can our species live in expanding waves of peace and prosperity, free from the pattern of messing things up when they are going well?

I owe my life to those questions. In the process of answering them, I was able to create the kind of life I had only dreamed about, as well as to help many others make their dreams come true. The discovery catapulted me out of an excellent life into an extraordinary place I had never imagined. We've got happy kids, we live in a house we love, and I haven't had to do anything I didn't want to do for so long I can't even remember what it feels like. If any or all of that sounds good to you, you're holding in your hands the way to make it happen for yourself.

Preparing for Your Big Leap

The One Problem and
How to Solve It

HOW TO BEGIN

If you would like to make your journey to the Zone of Genius smooth and rapid, please take a moment now to answer four questions. Start with this fundamental one:

Am I willing to increase the amount of time every day that I feel good inside?

When I use the phrase "feel good," I'm talking about a natural, inner sense of well-being that's not dependent on outside factors such as what you've eaten or what you might be doing. It's important to begin with a willingness to feel good inside, because there's no sense enhancing other parts of your life at the expense of your inner well-being. I'd like you to spend more and more time every day enjoying an organic, deep feeling of body/mind wellness. That's what I'd like you to say yes to, if you're so inclined.

If you said yes to increasing the amount of time you feel good inside, let's extend the question to the outer aspects of your life:

Am I willing to increase the amount of time that my whole life goes well?

When I use the phrase "whole life," I'm talking about your work, your relationships, your creative pursuits, and any other aspects that are central to your life. What I'd like for you, if you're willing, is for all of your life to flow more positively and easefully, for longer and longer periods of time.

If you said yes to those questions, consider going one step further than merely increasing that amount of time:

Am I willing to feel good and have my life go well all the time?

At first glance, you might ask who wouldn't say yes to all of these questions. Well, for many of us, the idea of all of this positive emotion seems far-fetched to begin with. It is easy for us to just assume that with the positive comes the negative. To that I say, "Why not get willing, and see what happens?" We humans have a long and wonderful history of transcending our beliefs about what's possible. In the early days of the steam-powered train, learned scientists urged capping the speed at thirty miles per hour because they believed that the human body exploded at speeds greater than that. Finally some brave people risked going beyond that limiting belief and found that they did not explode. I think we're approximately at that same stage of development with regard to our ability to feel good and have our lives go well. In my life I've discovered that if I cling to the notion that something's not possible, I'm arguing in favor of limitation. And if I argue for my limitations, I get to keep them. Ultimately we have to ask ourselves, "What's the payoff for arguing forcefully for our limitations?" In the case of the steam engine, scientists were trying to protect people from harm. The limiting belief was well-intentioned even though it was erroneous. From my experience with a lot of people, as well as myself, over the past few decades, I think we can put our minds at ease: being willing to feel naturally good and have our lives go well is not a safety hazard.

In my view, saying yes to that question is one of the most courageous actions a human being can take. In the face of so much evidence that life hurts and is fraught with adversity on all fronts, having a willingness to feel good and have life go well all the time is a genuinely radical act. Going into space is no longer radical; you can buy a ticket online. However, going into your inner depths, where your most deeply held beliefs about what's possible reside, counts in my book as a radical act. If we think it's even remotely possible to feel good all the time and have life go well all the time, we owe it to ourselves to find out how many of us can do it.

Feeling good and having your life go well are wonderful outcomes, and I hope you say yes to both of them. However, I think they are just stepping-stones and launchpads to something really spectacular! If you are willing to feel good and have things go well all the time, consider the ultimate step:

Are you willing to take the Big Leap to your ultimate level of success in love, money, and creative contribution?

MAYNARD'S BIG LEAP

Maynard Webb said yes, and his example inspires me to this day. When I first met Maynard, he was the chief operating officer of eBay, serving during the same time period in which Meg Whitman was CEO. Almost everyone knows about eBay and its phenomenal impact, but fewer people know that Maynard Webb was one of the main architects of its meteoric success. By the time I met Maynard, he had already earned the respect not only of the employees and shareholders of eBay, but also of the larger community of high-tech executives across the world. Yet in my view he was operating in his Zone of Excellence, not his Zone of Genius. He had already amassed a sizeable fortune and could easily have rested on the laurels of his accomplishments at eBay. That's not the way Maynard Webb operates, though.

He chose to confront his Upper Limit Problem and make the Big Leap into his Zone of Genius. He saw how staying within the world of eBay would be staying within his comfort zone. The comfort zone is no place for a person like Maynard Webb, and I hope not for you, either. Your true home, and Maynard's, is in the Zone of Genius. It's the only place where we can fully celebrate and express the gifts we've been given.

Maynard's Big Leap took him out of the comfortable niche that had made him wealthy and into the unknown of a new start-up company, Live Ops, which is revolutionizing the field of customer service. As CEO of Live Ops, Maynard has the pleasure of knowing that when he opens his office door every day, he is opening new territory in himself and in the world. He's using himself fully, using everything he's learned to make a bigger difference in the world.

Now, contrast Maynard's story with that of a person I didn't get to know until after he ran head-on into his Upper Limit. Dr. Richard Jordan had created a successful small business that attracted the attention of a larger firm. The firm made him an offer of three million dollars for his business, plus a generous two-year employment contract for himself. After weeks of negotiation, they were on the verge of signing the deal. Then one morning Dr. Jordan woke up with some last-minute concerns, the main one being that the new employment contract offered him two fewer weeks of vacation than he was used to taking. He got into an angry confrontation with the negotiator over this detail, which resulted in a letter from the company stating that "due to the force of your remarks," they were no longer interested in acquiring the business.

In a letter to me, Dr. Jordan said, "In that phone call I waved good-bye to three million dollars in cash, salary, and incentives." Fortunately, Dr. Jordan was able to learn from the experience. His letter continued: "Over the next few years I would awaken many nights with a knot in my stomach. Then I finally found the diamond in the dust. After much work and introspection, I discovered that what I was really saying to that man was 'Wait a minute! Three million dollars! That's way more than I'm worth. I cannot allow this!'" He decided to use the experience as, in his words, "the Three-Million-Dollar Gift." He formed two wonder questions to use in his life going forward:

How much love and abundance am I willing to allow?

How am I getting in my own way?

These questions cleared the way through his Upper Limit Problem, and ultimately he sold the business to another buyer. The story has a happy ending moneywise, but, more important, Dr. Jordan shows us how to turn dust into diamonds by understanding the Upper Limit Problem at work in this kind of situation. Another person might have continued to blame the other company or himself and gone on down that path to bitterness and despair. Instead, Dr. Jordan had the insight and courage to ask big questions and savor the big rewards that come along with them.

FOCUSING ON YOU

Now, turn your attention to yourself. Did you answer yes to those three questions I posed at the beginning of the chapter? If you did, you've taken the first crucial step in the journey. If you got a no or a maybe, let's explore why you might resist the idea.

When you consider the possibility of consistently feeling good and having things go well in your life all the time, you may find yourself thinking, "That's not possible." If so, I understand. I once felt that way, too. I urge you, though, not to waste much of your precious time worrying about whether it's possible. I've proven beyond the shadow of a doubt that it *is*. The only relevant question is whether *you* will let it be possible for *you*. If you would be willing to accept that possibility, you're on the way to experiencing real magic in your life.

I've asked thousands of people if they would be willing to feel good and have things go well all the time, and I've had the great joy of watching what happens in their lives when they say, *"Yes!"* I would love for you to enjoy the same results, and it all starts with a sincere *"Yes!"* to those three questions.

If you feel resistance and would like to explore it, you can begin by letting yourself know that it's quite natural to feel that way. After all, human beings have very little experience with consciously cultivating the ability to feel more and more positive energy. There wasn't a class in elementary school or college called "How to Tolerate Longer Periods of Success and Good Feeling." I think it's remarkable that we can go all the way from kindergarten to a Ph.D. or MD without anybody mentioning something so fundamental, but that's the world we live in at present. We're going to change that world, though, and we're going to reap phenomenal benefits from doing it.

There's an even bigger reason you might feel some resistance about transcending your Upper Limit Problem. Speaking personally, I found that my biggest resistance was the fear of owning my full potential. As I explored this fear, I realized that making such a big commitment put everything on the line. It eliminated any excuse I'd ever allowed myself for failing to achieve what I set out to do. In the past, I could always say, "Well, I failed, but I wasn't really trying hard. Maybe I'd have succeeded if I had really tried." Or "I failed, but I might have succeeded if I hadn't gotten sick." But now, after making the commitment to going the distance, any excuse that crept into my mind sounded hollow, even ridiculous, as if Columbus had sailed back to Europe and said, "Well, we didn't find land, but we might have if I hadn't gotten a nasty cold."

Many of our fears are based on the workings of the ego, the part of us that's focused on getting recognition and protecting us from social ostracism. In the Zone of Genius, your ego is unnecessary; living there is its own reward. In the Zone of Genius, you cease to care about recognition or ostracism. Once you make a commitment to inhabiting your full potential, your ego is suddenly faced with extinction. It's been making excuses for you throughout your life. Now, if your commitment to taking your Big Leap is sincere, your ego will need to be shown the door. Unless you're lucky, your ego will probably not go quietly. It has a lifetime of employment history behind it.

Faced with annihilation, your ego will set off a smoke bomb of fear. It will attempt to sabotage you by telling you tall tales of the terrors you'll experience if you take the Big Leap into your Zone of Genius. Using the smoke screen of fear as your own inner IMAX, it will project pictures of financial ruin and other disasters sure to befall you. All this is understandable, because fear is always about the unknown. This is unknown territory. Your ego has never been in this fix before. Ultimately, fear will be banished, because fear disappears when you're fully engaged in the Zone of Genius. Until you get there, though, you'll find yourself befogged more than once. Fortunately, this territory has been mapped out. There's something to help you find a way through, although it is probably unlike any navigational tool you've used in the past.

THE WAY THROUGH

There's only one way to get through the fog of fear, and that's to transform it into the clarity of exhilaration. One of the greatest pieces of wisdom I've ever heard comes from Fritz Perls, MD, the psychiatrist and founder of Gestalt therapy.

He said, "Fear is excitement without the breath." Here's what this intriguing statement means: the very same mechanisms that produce excitement also produce fear, and any fear can be transformed into excitement by breathing fully with it. On the other hand, excitement turns into fear quickly if you hold your breath. When scared, most of us have a tendency to try to get rid of the feeling. We think we can get rid of it by denying or ignoring it, and we use holding our breath as a physical tool of denial.

It never works, though, because as Dr. Perls has pointed out, the less breath you feed your fear, the bigger your fear gets. The best advice I can give you is to take big, easy breaths when you feel fear. Feel the fear instead of pretending it's not there. Celebrate it with a big breath, just the way you'd celebrate your birthday by taking a big breath and blowing out all the candles on your cake. Do that, and your fear turns into excitement. Do it more, and your excitement turns into exhilaration. I find it very empowering to know that I'm in charge of the exhilaration I feel as I go through life. I bet you will, too.

When you reach the end of your life and are wondering whether it's all been worthwhile, you'll be measuring whether you did everything you possibly could with the gifts you've been given. When I was growing up, my next-door neighbor Mr. Lewin shared a powerful bit of wisdom with me. I've kept it in mind for more than fifty years. On Judgment Day, Mr. Lewin said, God will not ask, "Why were you not Moses?"

He will ask, "Why were you not Sam Lewin?" The goal in life is not to attain some imaginary ideal; it is to find and fully use our own gifts. The meaning of that saying was clear even to a ten-year-old (who sends long-overdue thanks to Mr. Lewin, a successful seventy-year-old businessman when I knew him, for his willingness to shoot the breeze on many a Florida afternoon with a philosophically inclined kid).

MOVING BEYOND THE HARDEST PART

If you say yes to taking the Big Leap, you have done the hardest part. Your sincere commitment to going all the way to your Zone of Genius is the entry gate to the garden of miracles we will explore in this book. My intention is to show you exactly how to free yourself from the self-imposed limitation that is keeping you from your ultimate success. If you are already successful yet sense there is a quantum jump in your success that awaits you, you can take that quantum jump with the tools in this book. I guarantee it. That may sound like a bold claim, but this method has been taught to hundreds of people who were already achieving ordinary success and then took the Big Leap into the extraordinary. Later, we'll meet several of those people. Some of them are famous, some are not, but they all have one thing in common: they learned what I'm going to tell you about, and they transcended ordinary success to a level they hadn't imagined possible.

HOW THE UPPER LIMIT PROBLEM WORKS

Let me show you specifically how the Upper Limit Problem holds us back:

Each of us has an inner thermostat setting that determines how much love, success, and creativity we allow ourselves to enjoy. When we exceed our inner thermostat setting, we will often do something to sabotage ourselves, causing us to drop back into the old, familiar zone where we feel secure.

Unfortunately, our thermostat setting usually gets programmed in early childhood, before we can think for ourselves. Once programmed, our Upper Limit thermostat setting holds us back from enjoying all the love, financial abundance, and creativity that's rightfully ours. It keeps us in our Zone of Competence or at best our Zone of Excellence. It prevents us from living in the ultimate destination of the journey—our Zone of Genius. We'll explore these zones in more detail later in this chapter. For now, though, what you need to know is this: if you make a spectacular leap in one area of your life, such as money, your Upper Limit Problem quickly enshrouds you in a wet-wool blanket of guilt that keeps you from enjoying your new abundance. Guilt is a way our minds have of applying a painful grip on the conduit through which our good feelings flow.

In childhood, our Upper Limit Problem develops in acts of misguided altruism. Specifically, it develops with our attempts to take care of the feelings of others. Children are uncommonly skilled at reading body language. Perhaps you notice that the smile disappears from your mother's face when you outshine one of your siblings. You quickly learn to pull back a little from shining to take care of your mother's feelings. Many years later in adult life, you may find the very same pattern operating even though there is no mother around whose feelings you need to protect. In the next chapter, we'll explore in great detail the underlying mechanisms of the Upper Limit Problem.

A RADICAL IDEA

Take a close-up look at how guilt operates in conjunction with the Upper Limit Problem. It shows up when we're feeling good (or making extra money or feeling a deeper loving connection in a relationship). When we're feeling good, we may come up against the hidden barrier of an old belief such as "I must not feel good, because fundamentally flawed people like me don't deserve it." The churning froth of these two powerful forces clashing with each other is the chief constituent of the irritating, itchy, slow-drizzle feeling of guilt.

When the old belief clashes with the positive feelings you're enjoying, one of them has to win. If the old belief wins, you turn down the volume on the positive feeling (or lose some money or start an intimacy-destroying argument with your partner). If the good feeling wins, congratulations! Your practice in expanding your capacity for positive energy is paying off. Your capacity expands in small increments each time you consciously let yourself enjoy the money you have, the love you feel, and the creativity you are expressing in the world. As that capacity for enjoyment expands, so does your financial abundance, the love you feel, and the creativity you express.

Take a moment to appreciate how radical this idea is. Most people think they will finally feel good when they have more money, better relationships, and more creativity. I understand this point of view, because I felt that way half my life. What a powerful moment it is, though, when we finally see that we have it the wrong way around. All of us can find and nurture the capacity for positive feelings *now*, rather than waiting until some longed-for event occurs.

If you focus for a moment, you can always find some place in you that feels good right now. Your task is to give the expanding positive feeling your full attention. When you do, you will find that it expands with your attention. Let yourself enjoy it as long as you possibly can.

As you get more practice, you will be able to use this radical act of appreciation in other areas such as money and love. Instead of waiting to feel good until you have all the money you want and need, go ahead right now and appreciate your current money supply. All it takes is a few seconds. Find a place in yourself where you can feel good about the money you have. Give your full attention to that place of satisfaction. If you can't find any place in you where you feel good about money, create a positive thought about it in your mind. Float a new thought through your mind such as "I enjoy the money I have" or "I always have plenty of money to do everything I want to do."

Try it out in the area of love. Instead of focusing on loneliness or stagnation in a relationship, find a place in yourself where you can feel good about the love you have in your life. Give your full attention to that place of joy or satisfaction. Feel it expand as you give awareness to it. As you get more skilled with this practice, you discover that your positive feelings, your abundance, your love and creativity all begin to expand. Then, the outer aspects of your life change to match the expanding good feeling inside you.

Because few people understand how the Upper Limit Problem works, many of us believe we are flawed, not destined for greatness, or simply not good enough to deserve the dreams we want to achieve. Others miss out on big-time success and chalk it up to bad luck or bad timing. Millions of people are stuck on the verge of reaching their goals, can't seem to scale the wall, and are struggling under a glass ceiling that is completely within their control, waiting to be removed. But here's the good news: You're not flawed or unlucky or anything of the sort. You've got the Upper Limit Problem, and it can be transcended in the wink of an eye—if you're equipped with the right tools and a willing heart.

Here's a deeper look at how the Upper Limit Problem keeps us trapped: When you push through your Upper Limit thermostat setting by making more money, experiencing more love, or drawing more positive attention to yourself, you trip your Upper Limit switch. Deep inside your mind a little voice says, "You can't possibly feel this good" (or "make this much money" or "be this happy in love"). Unconsciously, you then do something to bring yourself back down to the thermostat setting you're familiar with. Even if you do achieve a glorious new height, it is often short-lived.

If you want some real-world evidence of the Upper Limit Problem in action, take a look at the studies of lottery winners. One study found that over 60 percent of them had blown the money within two years and returned to the same net worth as before their big win. Some were even worse off financially than before they won the lottery. Add to their financial woes the large number of divorces, family squabbles, and conflicts with friends that lottery winners often experience, and you have a classic example of the Upper Limit Problem at work. A man named Jack Whitaker, winner of more than three hundred million dollars in the Powerball lottery, has been extensively studied because of the litany of disasters that have befallen him after his big win. Here are some (but by no means all) of his post-win misfortunes: his wife left him; he was robbed of $545,000 cash when he passed out in a strip club; his granddaughter died of a drug overdose in his home; he has been arrested for drunk driving and assaulting a bartender; and he has had more than four hundred lawsuits brought against him by friends, family members, and others. Ironically, he was already a millionaire when he won the three hundred million dollars, so it is quite clear that the massive infusion of new wealth pushed him past his Upper Limit thermostat setting.

Each of us has an unconscious tendency to trip our Upper Limit switch, and each of us can eliminate that tendency. We deserve to experience wave after wave of greater love, creative energy, and financial abundance, without the compulsion to sabotage ourselves. That's what I want for you, and I hope that's what you want for yourself. If you want to eliminate your Upper Limit Problem—if you will make a commitment to clearing it out of your consciousness—you're more than halfway there.

THE UPPER LIMIT THERMOSTATS OF FAMOUS AND HIGHLY SUCCESSFUL PEOPLE

Once, as a young man, Bill Clinton stood in line to take a tour of the White House. He casually said to an attendant, "I am going to live here someday as president." And he achieved that goal. But then his Upper Limit Problem kicked in. He self-sabotaged his success by getting involved in a sex scandal that led to impeachment and disgrace. He failed to understand his Upper Limit Problem, and it kept him from enjoying fully his place in American history.

Here are a few more prominent examples of the Upper Limit Problem in action. John Belushi rose to enormous success quite rapidly; at his peak he had a number-one album, the top-grossing movie, and a hit TV show. Then, his Upper Limit Problem got him; he self-destructed as meteorically as he had risen. Then, there's Boris Becker, who won Wimbledon at the remarkable age of seventeen. Almost before the trophy was on the mantle, though, his Upper Limit Problem kicked in. He decided to fire his coach—the man who'd taken him to tennis greatness. The next year Boris hardly got in the door at Wimbledon before getting beat by the seventy-first-ranked player. The actor Christian Bale starred in the Batman movie *The Dark Knight*, which had one of the most profitable openings in movie history. In London for the movie's premiere, he got into an altercation in his hotel room (with his mother and sister, no less) and ended up with assault charges filed against him.

People often experience big breakthroughs . . . and then find a way to avoid relishing their achievement. They receive an award at work and then have a screaming argument with their spouse later that same night. They get the job of their dreams and then get sick; they win the lottery, then have an accident. The newfound success trips their Upper Limit switch, and they plummet back to the familiar setting they've grown used to.

My wife, Kathlyn, and I have enjoyed Bonnie Raitt's company as a friend, and have celebrated her evolution as an artist, for close to twenty years. She is a great living example of how to find your ultimate success by taking the Big Leap. Although she lives securely now in her Zone of Genius, her path to get there was long and arduous. In the first part of her career, Bonnie earned an excellent reputation as a blues musician. Her blues albums were seldom best sellers, but they always did well enough to keep her devoted fans happy and the clubs full. Like many of her idols in the blues lineage, though, she paid her dues by years of struggle with addictions. Battling her demons consumed a great deal of her energy, and it wasn't until she got sober that she made her Big Leap. Two of her best friends, Stevie Ray Vaughan and John Hiatt, inspired her by kicking their addictions and succeeding in Twelve-Step programs. Finally she made the commitment to get clean and sober, and that's when the real magic began.

With the new energy and clarity she gained through sobriety, Bonnie took a look at her career and made a fateful decision. She decided to jump out of the trap of "Excellent Blues Musician." She made a conscious choice to launch herself into the bigger world of mainstream rock music. She was hearing songs inside herself that didn't fit into the traditional themes, rhythms, and keys of the blues. So, she said a loving good-bye to the friendly confines of the blues world and took the Big Leap into the unknown. She recorded an album of the new music and went on the road with a new band. In her meditations, she visualized herself onstage at the Grammy Awards, receiving the accolades of the music industry for the new music. She even visualized the specific dress she would wear when she received the award. Not long afterward, she was standing onstage receiving a Grammy for that new album, *Nick of Time,* which went on to sell millions of copies. Now, nine Grammys, sold-out stadiums, and millions of albums later, she is living testimony to the power of claiming your Zone of Genius.

It took a Big Leap on her part to go from clubs to stadiums, but she took that risk and has reaped incredible rewards. Beyond all the Grammy Awards and other material benefits, though, is an achievement that's purely a gift to the soul: the deep satisfaction of living in her Zone of Genius. That's what I want you to experience. You know deep inside you that you will never be fully satisfied until you have anchored yourself in your Zone of Genius. To do less would be to hold back, and long ago you made a handshake deal with the universe that you wouldn't do that. The seductive comforts of success, though, can lull us into accepting the status quo. In that state of comfort, it's easy to forget the deal you made with the universe to use yourself fully.

SOLVING ONE PROBLEM AND FREEING YOURSELF

By its very nature, the Upper Limit Problem is unsolvable in your ordinary state of consciousness. If you could solve it that way, you would have solved it long ago. Solving the Upper Limit Problem is possible only by a leap of consciousness. Once you learn this way to solve problems, you'll have a tool you can apply wherever and whenever you want to increase your success.

Specifically, the Upper Limit Problem cannot be solved in the usual way we solve problems: by gathering information or replacing one set of information with another. The Upper Limit Problem must be *dis*-solved, not solved. You dissolve it by shining a laserlike beam of awareness on its underpinnings—the false foundations that hold the Upper Limit Problem in place. When you shine the light of awareness on the underpinnings, they disappear. Then you are free to soar, explore, and rest at home in the no-limits zone of your ultimate success.

Our activities in the world occur in four main zones:

The Zone of Incompetence

The Zone of Incompetence is made up of all the activities we're not good at. Others can do them a lot better than we can. Surprisingly, many successful people persist in wasting time and energy doing things for which they have no talent. When you focus awareness on yourself by using the tools in this book, you may be surprised to find how much time you spend operating in this zone. When you free yourself from this zone, you will be rewarded with a remarkable new feeling of energy and zest for living.

The best way to handle most things in your Zone of Incompetence is to avoid doing them altogether. Delegate them to someone else, or find some other creative way to avoid doing them. I got a call one Sunday night from a friend of mine,

Thomas, a business consultant with whom I play golf from time to time. He told me he'd spent a frustrating weekend installing a new thousand-dollar printer at his home. Most frustrating to him was the four hours he'd spent on the phone with the technical-support people at Hewlett-Packard. I happen to know that he is just about as unskilled as I am at mechanical things. I also know that he bills his consulting time at ten thousand dollars a day. His hourly rate for over-the-phone executive coaching is one thousand dollars an hour.

I asked him how many hours in total he'd spent wrestling with the new printer. "Thirteen," he said, sounding a bit sheepish. "Hmmm," I said, "you spent thirteen thousand dollars trying to install a one-thousand-dollar printer. Did you ever get it working?" "No," he said, "I eventually called a college kid in the neighborhood. He came over and got it working in an hour." "And you paid him how much?" I asked. Thomas said, "At first he didn't want anything, but I made him take a hundred bucks."

I forgot to mention that his frustrating Saturday had been capped off that evening by an argument with his wife. You can probably guess what the argument was about: all the hours he was spending on the printer installation instead of with her and the family. Add that cost to the thirteen thousand dollars, plus the hundred-dollar "service" tab, and you have an expensive excursion in the Zone of Incompetence.

One thing I've learned from a lifetime of observing: being smart doesn't keep you from doing dumb things. My grandfather had a colorful phrase he used: "stuck on stupid." It meant that you kept doing the same dumb things over and over without learning from them. I felt a bit like that when I first realized how much time and energy got consumed when I was doing things I was not good at. It's worthwhile to do something you're not good at if the intention is to enjoy or master it. Skiing was like that for me. I grew up in Florida and never saw a snowflake in person until I was twenty-three years old. My first outing on skis was probably laughable viewed from the outside, but from the inside it was memorably painful. I fell so many times that when I got home that night I felt like I'd been hit repeatedly by a bus. It was worth it, though, because I wanted to enjoy skiing someday.

For my friend Thomas, spending all weekend fretting over a printer did not come from an intention of someday mastering printer installation. In his words, it came from "trying to save a few bucks."

The Zone of Competence

You're competent at the activities in the Zone of Competence, but others can do them just as well. Successful people often discover that they expend far too much time and energy in this zone. Not long ago I worked with a woman in her mid-forties who contributes a classic example of the Competence Trap. An executive in a small firm, Joan was referred to me by her medical doctor, who felt that some of her health issues were due to what I sometimes call "diseases of unfulfill-ment." When people are not expressing their full potential, they often get illnesses that have vague, hard-to-diagnose symptoms. Chronic fatigue syndrome and fibromyalgia are good examples of what I'm describing. I've seen both of those illnesses disappear when people began to break out of their sub-Genius zones and move toward fulfilling their true potential. In the course of several sessions, Joan moved from talking about chronic fatigue syndrome to telling me about a workplace frustration that had recycled for several years. Because she was good at organizing things, she got called on more and more to handle tasks outside her job description, from the company picnic to the travel schedules of the other executives. "One of the executive assistants could do those kinds of things," she told me, "but I end up doing them be-cause it's quicker to do it myself than to delegate and follow up on them." I asked her, "If you could stop doing that sort of thing, what would it free up time for you to do?" She men-tioned a few activities, but none of them produced any ex-pressions of liveliness or excitement on her face. I asked her to go a little deeper: "If money or your job description were not an issue, what would you really like to be doing in the company?" Here we struck gold. "I wouldn't be doing any-thing in the company," she said. "I'd be working on an en-vironmental project I'm obsessed with. I think it could turn into something big, but there's a big gap between thinking that and making a living at it." That admission turned the key. We made a plan that first called for her to eliminate the extra organizational tasks that kept her in her Zone of Competence. It took her a couple of weeks to extricate herself and delegate those tasks to others. Just taking that initial step cleared up most of her physical symptoms. She felt so much better that the second part of the plan took an unexpected turn in a new direction. She decided to cut back to half time at the company and devote her newfound energy to working on the environmental project. Time will tell if she can stake out a life in her Zone of Genius, but at least she is not carrying the burden of unfulfillment and its attendant symptoms.

The Zone of Excellence

In the Zone of Excellence are the activities you do extremely well. You make a good living in your Zone of Excellence. For successful people, this zone is a seductive and even dangerous trap. To remain in this zone is to hobble yourself from taking the leap into your Zone of Genius. The temptation is strong to remain in the Zone of Excellence; it's where your own addiction to comfort wants you to stay. It's also where your family, friends, and organization want you to stay. You're reliable there, and you provide a steady supply of all the things that family, friends, and organizations thrive on. The problem is that a deep, sacred part of you will wither and die if you stay inside your Zone of Excellence. There is only one place where you will ultimately thrive and feel satisfied, and that's . . .

The Zone of Genius

Liberating and expressing your natural genius is your ultimate path to success and life satisfaction. Your Zone of Genius is the set of activities you are uniquely suited to do. They draw upon your special gifts and strengths. Your Zone of Genius beckons you with increasingly strong calls as you go through your life. (*The Call to Genius* is the name I've given to these inner promptings.) By age forty, many of us have tuned out the Call to Genius and are getting loud, repeated alarms hidden in the form of depression, illness, injuries, and relationship conflict. These alarms are reminding us to spend more time feeding our natural genius and letting it do its magic in the world. In this book I will show you how to heed this call and move gently and gracefully into your Zone of Genius.

I use the phrase "gently and gracefully" for a particular reason. If we don't heed the call and make a gentle, graceful move into our Zone of Genius, we often get painful life whacks that tell us with blatant clarity that we're not paying attention to the Call.

I recall a coaching conversation with Bill, a brilliant forty-three-year-old entrepreneur, who had been turning a deaf ear to his Call to Genius for far too long. He came in for one session, in which he told me about the bind he was in. Bill wanted passionately to pursue a certain new project, but he said he couldn't do it because of pressure from his company, his wife, and others. He said they could not afford to have him take the several months necessary to work on the new idea. As he described the new project, I could tell it was clearly in his Zone of Genius. I counseled Bill to do whatever it took to make it happen, even if he could spend only an hour a day laying the groundwork for it. At the end of the session he told me he was going to "try" to find that hour a day, but I could tell by the look on his face that it was unlikely to occur. He told me he would call me in a month to schedule a second appointment "when things slowed down a little." It was our last conversation, because Bill died of a massive heart attack a few weeks later.

I have replayed that hour with him in my mind more times than I can count. Bill was seemingly in perfect health. His wife was a yoga teacher; they were both devoted to a healthy lifestyle. I've always wondered if there was a way in which I could have been more forceful with him in helping him make a life-changing, and possibly life-saving, commitment to his Zone of Genius. I'll never know, but from that experience I made a commitment to myself to do everything I could to spend more time in my own Zone of Genius, and to make a passionate case to everyone I care about to do the same.

Given the right tools and a little wisdom, we can learn to heed our Call to Genius, sparing ourselves the unpleasant consequences of plugging our ears to keep from hearing it. The book shows you how to establish yourself in your Zone of Genius, beginning with a modest investment of ten minutes a day and culminating in spending upwards of 70 percent of your time expressing your true genius in the world. I hit the 70 percent mark in the mid-nineties, and rebirthed myself at midlife into a previously unimaginable degree of success in love, financial abundance, and creativity. That's what I want for you. If that's what *you* want for you, you will find precise tools here for identifying your natural genius and expressing it in the world.

Making the Leap

Dismantling the Foundation of the Problem

There is something important you should know about the Upper Limit Problem: when you attain higher levels of success, you often create personal dramas in your life that cloud your world with unhappiness and prevent you from enjoying your enhanced success. This is the Upper Limit Problem at work. In other words, the Upper Limit Problem crosses the boundaries of money, love, and creativity. If you make more money, your Upper Limit Problem may kick in and create a situation that causes unhappiness, ill health, or something else that blocks your enjoyment of your enhanced money supply. If you meet and marry the love partner of your dreams, your Upper Limit Problem may kick in and cause setbacks in your financial life. In short, you have a tendency to follow big leaps forward in your success with big mess-ups.

These mess-ups rubber-band you back to where you were before, or sometimes some place worse. Fortunately, though, if you see what you're doing in time, you can shift right out of the free fall and point yourself back up toward the sky.

See if any of these scenarios sound familiar:

You make a big financial surge forward, such as a big stock-market win or something else that causes a meaningful financial change. Almost before you've had a chance to celebrate, an argument or an illness or some other negative occurrence throws a wet blanket on the good feelings.

You're feeling close to your love partner. Perhaps you're sitting together quietly, sipping a glass of your favorite wine. Seemingly out of nowhere, an argument sparks into flame. The close feelings disappear; you're embroiled in a conflict that stretches into hours or maybe even days.

You're sitting alone in your office or your living room. You feel happy and at ease. Suddenly your mind swerves and plunges into a stream of negative thoughts. Seconds later you're obsessing about the awful condition of the world or focusing on the dreadful color of your carpets.

Let me give you a more specific example. I assisted a powerful, wealthy businesswoman in making a breakthrough in the area of romantic relationships. In her mid-fifties when I worked with her, Lois told me in our first session that she could "do just about anything well except stay married." Twice-divorced and now single for five years, she despaired of finding and keeping a good relationship. She even recited statistics: her odds of being captured by terrorists were better than her chances of finding love at her age. Lois was quite stubborn in clinging to her views, so it took us a few sessions to unwind the set of limiting beliefs she clung to around the availability of men. Finally she realized that it didn't matter if men were scarce: all she needed was one. In a pivotal session, she made a firm, heartfelt commitment to attracting and keeping a healthy, loving relationship with a man.

At the beginning of the following week she called to cancel her next session. She said she had met a wonderful man two days after our last session and had spent the most romantic weekend of her life with him. She thanked me for helping her make this shift and said she didn't need any more help. I gently suggested that this was just the time she should come in. I explained that while breakthroughs are important and thrilling, it's the subsequent stabilization and integration of the breakthrough into daily life that really allow the changes to be permanent. She listened politely, said, "Thank you," and hung up without making another appointment.

About six months later I got an urgent message to call her. When I reached her, I could hardly understand her because she was talking so fast. I invited her to slow her breathing down, which helped her get her anxiety dialed down to a level at which she could communicate clearly. She told me that her new husband, the man she'd spent the glorious weekend with the last time I'd spoken to her, had counseled her on an investment that had lost over two hundred thousand dollars virtually overnight. He'd had some "inside information" on a stock that was supposed to go up and instead went down. The "sure thing" that was going to double her money overnight instead wiped it out completely.

"What should I do?" she asked. "Should I throw him out or leave or—"

"Hold on," I said. "Has he ever done anything like this before?"

"No," she said.

"And what's his behavior been like over the past few months?"

"Wonderful," she said. "I've never been happier in my life, until this happened."

"And what does he do for work?"

"He's a software designer. He consults for different high-tech companies."

"So, does he make a good living doing that?"

"Pretty good," she said. "But he's kind of a frugal person. He doesn't need a huge income."

"Let me ask you a question," I said. "What gave you the idea you should take investment advice from him?"

There was a long silence. Finally she said "Oh, my God."

"What's happening?" I asked.

"I just realized that I love him so much it never occurred to me that he was flawed."

I asked her to reconsider the judgment that he was "flawed." I told her: "He's not necessarily flawed. *You're* the savvy businessperson who chose to take investment advice from a software designer."

In the ensuing silence I could almost hear Lois's teeth grinding. Finally she said, "Damn you, you're right. And do you know how many times in my life I've said that?"

I hazarded a guess: "Never?" Again she uttered the magic phrase: "You're right. Zero. I can't remember ever admitting somebody else was right."

I suggested that it might be a useful skill to learn if she wanted to have a happy marriage. I told her that I had found it a great addition to my own communication repertoire. On the occasions when I said, "You're right" in my own marriage, I noticed that Kathlyn responded as if she were hearing the sweet sounds of a Mozart concerto.

Lois and her husband came in for a session together. It turned out that he not only loved her very much but was also very intimidated by her. To make up for his perceived inadequacy, he wanted to impress her in her own area of expertise. This muddled intention had caused him to present the stock tip he'd heard as if it were a sure thing. Like many muddled intentions, it produced the opposite effect.

Toward the end of the session I asked a question that can shine a light on an Upper Limit Problem: "Lois, why do you think this money incident happened at this particular time in your life?"

Long silence. Finally she said, "I think I got happier than I ever imagined I could be. Then some part of me reared up and grabbed me—some part of me that didn't think I deserved it. I created this drama with Larry to find something wrong with him, to give me an excuse to end the relationship. All because I think I don't deserve to be this happy."

"So," I said, "let's make a new deal between you and the universe right now. Are you willing to be wealthy in both money *and* love?" She took a deep breath and said, "Yes!"

I complimented her on her insight and her willingness to make a new commitment to feeling fulfilled in both financial and romantic terms.

Lois offers a beautiful example of how to handle the Upper Limit Problem. She came right up to the brink of sabotaging a good relationship, but she caught herself in time. She was even able to use the incident as a time of deepening her connection with her husband. Six months into a close relationship is about when the big issues begin to surface. At that point, most of us don't say, "Oh, I'm about six months into this wonderful relationship. It's about time for my big issues to come up and cause me to sabotage the relationship." Instead, most of us go to the opposite extreme: we herald this time of deepening by seeing a fault or flaw in the other person, then studying it so microscopically that it expands into a vast new field of scientific inquiry.

Here's a new way: when the big stuff comes up, ask your partner if she or he is willing to join you as an equal partner on a learning journey. If the answer is yes, you join together in a relationship of true possibility. If she or he is more committed to being right than to actual, real intimacy, the answer will be something other than yes. Then you must move on, and be quick about it.

Now, though, let's return to the central issue: how the Upper Limit Problem works, and how to eliminate its negative effects on us.

TRIGGERING THE UPPER LIMIT PROBLEM

The false foundation under the Upper Limit Problem is a set of four hidden barriers based on fear and false belief. Every person I've worked with has uncovered at least one of the barriers, and sometimes two or three. I've never met anybody who had all four. The Four Hidden Barriers all have something in common: although they seem true and real, they are based on beliefs about ourselves that are neither true nor real. The fact that *we unconsciously take them as true and real* is the barrier holding us back. We take them as true and real until we shine awareness on them. Then the barriers dissolve, and we are free. That moment is profound. It feels wonderful; we remember it forever. It is the occasion of our ultimate liberation. Although I have myself experienced that joyful moment and have witnessed it hundreds of times, I am still deeply moved every time it occurs.

Begin by considering the possibility that you have at least one hidden barrier that is keeping you from being completely successful. Please know that you're far from alone. I had more than one. Even if you're already very successful, you have at least one barrier that holds you back. When you encounter the barrier, your Upper Limit Problem is triggered. The form it takes depends on which fears and false beliefs you picked up in your early life. As we explore those fears and false beliefs now, tune in to discover which ones resonate with your experience.

Four fears and four related false beliefs hold the Upper Limit Problem in place. The fears are based on specific long-ago situations you will probably recognize when I show them to you. The beliefs based on those fears are false and cause you to have a misunderstanding about who you actually are. These fears and false beliefs cause us to live our lives out of a success-limiting mantra that says:

I cannot expand to my full potential because _____

_____

_____.

In relationships, your Upper Limit mantra says:

I cannot enjoy abundant love and relationship harmony because _____.

In financial wealth, your Upper Limit mantra says:

I cannot expand to my full wealth potential because _____

_____.

When you remove those false beliefs, you feel a new freedom to invent a life based on your natural genius. I now want to describe the fears and false beliefs, with the intention of assisting you in dissolving and dismantling them.

Hidden Barrier no. 1: Feeling Fundamentally Flawed

A feeling that I'm fundamentally flawed in some way. That's how one of my clients, Carl, described the barrier of feeling fundamentally flawed, and we can use his phrase as a definitive example of the most pervasive of the Hidden Barriers. Let's dismantle it piece by piece, so you can see how it got a grip on Carl. Find out if his story resonates with your own. His Upper Limit mantra went like this:

I cannot expand to my full creative genius because something is fundamentally wrong with me.

If you have a deep, old feeling that there's something wrong, bad, or flawed about you, you will find yourself grappling with that issue every time you break through to greater love and financial abundance. When you surpass your Upper Limit thermostat setting, a little voice admonishes you from deep within your mind: you should not be this happy (or rich or creative) because you are fundamentally flawed. This thought creates cognitive dissonance, the mind rattle that occurs when you try to hold two opposing thoughts at the same time: *Given that I am fundamentally flawed (or wrong or bad), how can I possibly be this happy, rich, and creative?* The cognitive dissonance must be resolved in one of two ways: by returning to your previous thermostat setting; or by letting go of the old, limiting belief, which allows you to stabilize at the new, higher level.

The best way is to shine the light of awareness on the thought that you are fundamentally flawed and label it as what it is: an Upper Limit bug. I use *bug* in two senses here. It's like a computer bug, because it's a false line in your code that causes a breakdown in your operating efficiency. It's like a bug in the mosquito sense, too, because it bites you when you are going to higher levels of love, abundance, and creativity. You start slapping at the bug and bring yourself back down to your previous level.

The other way to stop the cognitive dissonance is to pull back from your success and not challenge the false belief. This move brings you back down into a zone you're familiar with. The bug wins, and you lose.

In Carl's case it was easy to see where he picked up his bug, the feeling of being fundamentally flawed. He had started out his life as the first child of a powerful executive who would go on to run two different Fortune 500 companies. When my client was just out of diapers, though, his parents split up and got into an epic battle over money, a conflict that went on for years. His father remarried and started another family, so Carl's early life was spent shuttling back and forth between these hostile forces. Later, in a moment of alcohol-induced candor, his father confessed to Carl that he could never look at him without simultaneously feeling hatred for Carl's mother. The father had convicted Carl of a crime Carl couldn't understand or name. All he knew was that his father looked at him differently than his younger half brother. Carl unconsciously convicted himself of the crime, too. Years later he would tell me, "I figured if he looked at me that way, I must have done something wrong, but I could never get anybody to tell me exactly what I'd done."

This next point is crucial: The invisible crime for which Carl was serving time had absolutely nothing to do with Carl. The father would have felt the same way about any child who occupied that role. You can see, though, how Carl (and the rest of us who have been in similar situations) would take it personally. After all, he was the one receiving the looks of misplaced hatred from his father. At two years of age (or five or fifteen), Carl had no way of knowing that the look was directed primarily at his mother. He had no way of knowing that he was completely innocent of the crime of which he'd been convicted.

The fear of being fundamentally flawed brings with it a related fear. It's the fear that if you did make a full commitment to living in your Zone of Genius, you might fail. It's the belief that even your genius is flawed, and that if you expressed it in a big way, it wouldn't be good enough. This belief tells you to play it safe and stay small. That way, if you fail, at least you fail small.

Hidden Barrier no. 2: Disloyalty and Abandonment

When we are stuck behind the barrier of disloyalty and abandonment, our unconscious mantra goes like this:

I cannot expand to my full success because it would cause me to end up all alone, be disloyal to my roots, and leave behind people from my past.

If you're wondering what kind of person might have a barrier like this, I can tell you: my kind of person, for one. This barrier caused me much consternation earlier in my life, and even now it still flickers through my mind from time to time. I'll tell you more about my story in a moment, but for now, focus on whether this barrier has shown up in your life. Here are two questions that can help you discover if you, too, have this barrier:

Did I break the family's spoken or unspoken rules to get where I am?

Even though I am successful, did I fail to meet the expectations my parents had of me?

If you answered yes to either of these questions, you're likely to feel guilty later as you expand into more and more success. You're likely to feel, at a deep and unconscious level, that your quest for a life of your own and success on your own terms has come at the cost of leaving behind your roots and being disloyal to those who loved you. The guilt you feel makes you put on the brakes, holding yourself back from ultimate success and keeping you from enjoying the success you already have. You follow breakthroughs of success with bouts of self-punishment.

Here's a vivid example of Hidden Barrier no. 2 in action:

I counseled a newlywed couple just after they'd had a memorable encounter with this barrier. Robert had just finished his medical residency; Dee was an administrator at the university where Robert had received his MD. Their backgrounds couldn't have been more different. Robert was from an "old money" family in New England, whereas Dee had been raised in a hippie enclave near Santa Cruz by a single mom. Robert's family didn't approve of Dee because she was five years older than Robert and didn't come from aristocratic stock. They probably would have disapproved even more had they known that Dee's mother also made her living by growing exotic herbs, some of which are illegal to possess. Nevertheless, Robert and Dee were deeply in love, and preliminary plans were made for a fancy wedding at the estate of Robert's family. On the insistence of Robert's family, the wedding was not to take place until after Robert got his first job as a physician.

In a mood of euphoria the day Robert completed his residency, they made a snap decision to do things their own way. They drove to Reno and got married in a wedding chapel. Without pausing even for lunch, they turned the car around and headed toward Santa Cruz. Dee's mother, Dorothy, was delighted when they called her with the news, and promised to arrange a big party that night to celebrate the wedding. Robert and Dee decided to postpone calling his family to tell them the good news.

As they navigated the winding dirt road toward Dorothy's cabin, Robert and Dee had an impulse to pull the car into the woods for a pre-party cuddle. They spread a blanket in the woods and fell to celebrating their first married lovemaking adventure. In the heat of passion, they rolled off the blanket into a bed of poison oak. Poison oak can take twenty-four hours to produce symptoms, so they didn't realize they were a ticking time bomb of red and itchy rash. They proceeded to the party, where Dorothy and her friends provided a raucous welcome to the newlyweds. After dancing and singing into the wee hours, they collapsed into bed, only to awaken the next morning with a double-barreled dose of misery: not only were they hung over; they were aflame with rash and itch. They spent the next few days in and out of ice-cube baths, imbibing pain relievers and slathering on lotion. Robert, up until then a teetotaler, even took comfort in some of Dorothy's exotic herbal preparations.

When they came in to talk to me a few weeks later, they were trying to make sense of this experience, but the sense they were making of it was not making them happy. Dee, looking through the cosmic-colored lenses of her upbringing, wondered if the experience was a sign from the universe that they shouldn't be together at all. Robert's view was purely self-critical. "I've treated cases of poison oak," he said. "Why the hell didn't I notice what we were rolling around in?" As I listened to their story I saw a flashing neon sign that read Barrier no. 2, and when I explained to them how it worked, I could see relief flooding into their faces.

Beyond giving them insight into why they had punished themselves so visibly and painfully, I also prescribed a radical treatment and offered them the equipment to carry it out on the spot. I handed them my telephone and invited them to call Robert's parents, who still hadn't been informed that their beloved son had wandered off the straight and narrow. They embraced this idea about as enthusiastically as a wild horse being offered a saddle for the first time. Therapists are prepared for such moments, though, and I convinced them that the longer they waited, the more difficult it would become.

Behind every communication problem is a sweaty ten-minute conversation you don't want to have. However, the moment you work up the courage to have it, you collect an instant reward in relief as well as open up a flow of communication that will allow you to resolve the situation. I listened as Robert and Dee broke the news and spoke their hearts to Robert's parents. After the first few minutes of uproar back and forth, the conversation turned harmonious and ended up with an invitation to have a big reception in New England rather than a wedding.

Hidden Barrier no. 3: Believing That More Success Brings a Bigger Burden

An old belief that you're a burden can hold you back from expanding to your full capacity for success and enjoyment. If this belief has a grip on you, your Upper Limit mantra goes like this:

> I can't expand to my highest potential because I'd be an even bigger burden than I am now.

Early on in our exploration I mentioned that it's common for people to have more than one hidden barrier. In my work on myself, I found that two of the barriers held the biggest challenge for me. In the last section I shared my challenges with overcoming the disloyalty and abandonment barrier. Now I want to tell you about the burden barrier, my second major challenge. Check to see if elements of my story resonate with you.

The moment I made my appearance in the world, I was greeted with two big mixed messages: you're a burden; and you're a celebration. I was a burden to my mother, but a cause for celebration to my grandparents. The reason I was a burden was that my father had died a few weeks after my conception, leaving my mother with three hundred dollars, my older brother to raise, and, unbeknownst to anyone, me in the womb. Mom had no job and would have had a struggle supporting herself and my six-year-old brother. The unexpected appearance of a new baby was more than the poor widow could handle, and she went into a depression for about a year after I was born. Fortunately, my grandparents were next door, both vital sixty-somethings, and they were beyond ecstatic about having a baby boy around. They had raised four daughters and were more than ready for a boy. I became the boy they'd always wanted, and there was never a day throughout my childhood that I didn't feel their love and caring attention. Having them next door was a godsend, even after my mother recovered and I began to spend more time at her house.

This background is a perfect setup for an Upper Limit Problem later in life. Starting out my life as a combination of burden and celebration caused me to repeat this combination often in adult life. I would have a big positive breakthrough, then immediately start feeling I was a burden on the world. Sometimes the world would pick up on my feeling and present immediate proof that I was indeed a burden.

I recall a painful moment, when I was in my late twenties, at a family gathering with my mother and brother. My first published book had just come out, and I'd brought a copy of it along for each of them. They were sitting at a table chatting when I proudly presented their books. Each of them looked at it, turned it this way and that, then put it aside without opening it or saying a word of congratulations. Then they resumed their conversation as if nothing had happened. I remember standing there dumbfounded. I didn't know about the Upper Limit Problem at the time, so it didn't occur to me that this event was part of a pattern set in motion long before I took my first breath. It took me years to understand what a burden upon them my existence must have been. I can't imagine the struggles they went through trying to cope with my unexpected appearance in their world. It's not surprising they would convict me of the crime of being a burden, so it's not surprising they would consider a book written by me as a burden upon their world. If their perception of me was that I'm a burden, they would naturally see anything I produced as a further burden. What's surprising is the extent to which I had convicted myself of that crime, even though I was innocent of the original imagined transgression.

By my thirties I began to wake up and realize that most of the guilt I felt was for crimes I hadn't committed. I bet you'll find the same thing. Of course, there are plenty of things I've done on my own that I feel guilty about. I imagine you can think of a few of those, too. However, I've found that if we remove the guilt of the crimes our parents and siblings convicted us of before we walked into kindergarten, we are liberated from the main issues that trigger the Upper Limit Problem.

Hidden Barrier no. 4: The Crime of Outshining

The unconscious mantra of the outshining barrier goes like this:

> I must not expand to my full success, because if I did I would outshine _____ and make him or her look or feel bad.

This barrier is very common among gifted and talented children. They get a lot of their parents' attention, but they also get a strong subliminal message along with it: don't shine too much, or you'll make others feel bad or look bad. The gifted child is often convicted of stealing attention from other members of the family. One unconscious solution gifted children devise is to turn down the volume on their genius so the others don't feel threatened by it. The other solution is to continue to shine brightly but turn down the volume on their enjoyment of it. If they can appear to be suffering, they can get empathy and sympathy from others instead of jealousy.

Kenny Loggins is a role model for how to transcend this barrier and take the Big Leap. Kenny has been a friend and neighbor for many years, and I've gone out on tour with him several times to serve as an on-the-road coach for him and the band. A few years ago I also worked with Kenny and his old partner, Jim Messina, in preparation for a reunion tour. Loggins and Messina conquered the world of rock music at an early age, attaining fame, fortune, and critical acclaim in their early twenties. Turmoil and creative clashes eventually caused them to break up, and trouble followed them into their solo careers. Kenny found success as a solo artist, with a string of hits in the eighties, while Jim tried different avenues such as producing albums for other musicians. Even though Kenny was cranking out hits and winning Grammys, he didn't let himself enjoy his success. When he would have a hit or win an award, he would do something in his personal life to sabotage the potential good feeling and celebration. He would get sick, or have an accident, or mess up a relationship; there was always something, and it was always just after a success of some sort. In working with Kenny extensively, and with Jim briefly, I discovered a classic example of Hidden Barrier no. 4.

Although they had never noticed it, they had a remarkable similarity in their backgrounds. They had grown up as gifted children trying to compete with a favored sibling for their parents' attention. They also got hidden messages from their parents not to outshine the other sibling. When the talented duo formed their musical union in their late teens, this early programming worked to their advantage. They were brother figures together, out to conquer the world. They could both shine together. And shine they did, with one hit after another.

However, when the time came to go solo and follow their own musical paths, the old Upper Limit Problem came back with full force. Now they were both in the grip of the old fear not to outshine the other one. This fear caused one to stumble in search of a new direction and the other to dampen the enjoyment of his success with one unfortunate incident of self-sabotage after another.

Fortunately, they woke up in time. They were able to spot this old pattern and transcend it. Jim launched a new career teaching songwriting workshops. Kenny got the gift of a seeming performance disaster that had a life-changing gift of a metaphor hidden in it. He was nominated for a Grammy, and at the awards show, with most of the music industry in attendance, he took the stage to sing the big hit "I'm All Right." Thunderous applause greeted the distinctive opening notes of the song, but in a masterpiece of irony, when Kenny started to sing the vocal, the microphone didn't work. He saved the moment by jumping on a table and leading an a cappella version until the mike got fixed, but the irony gave him cause for reflection later: why had he "lost" his voice at the very peak of his career? The answer led to his Big Leap and the creation of a masterpiece. He realized that he didn't want to create more of the same kind of staple pop hits that had made him rich and famous. Those were clearly in his Zone of Excellence, but clearly not in his Zone of Genius. Although he was proud of the pop hits he'd created, he felt that they still came out of that fear of outshining. Fortunately, he heeded the call of genius and went into a time of deep meditative inquiry about every aspect of his life. In that deep space he heard a new kind of music coming from within him, songs that touched on the environment, honesty in relationships, and other themes unusual in popular music. The album that emerged had a title appropriate to the role it played in his life: *Leap of Faith*. It was a massive hit both commercially and critically, and contained songs such as "Conviction of the Heart," which became an anthem of the growing environmentalist movement. This in turn led Kenny to a performance moment that eclipsed any thrill of the past: singing "Conviction of the Heart" to five hundred thousand people at an Earth Day celebration in Washington, D.C.

One great thing about Upper Limit work is that it doesn't take much time to spot where the problem is coming from. Once you see it, you've turned on a light in a long-dark room. There's cleanup work that usually needs to be done, but with the light on, it's not that hard.

A hex is often put on gifted and talented people early in life. The hex causes them to feel bad when they shine especially brightly. Why would parents hex children this way? An example will explain:

I worked with Joseph, a middle-aged executive who had been a piano prodigy as a child. He went on to modest success as a professional musician but then quit music completely because, without realizing it, he kept running up against Hidden Barrier no. 4. Specifically, each time Joseph had a breakthrough to more success, he would be gripped by guilt and end up feeling worse than before. Even after he quit music, the pattern followed him into his business career.

During our first session we were able to shine a light on the moment in his past when the barrier first got locked into place. Growing up, Joseph had been close to his only other sibling, a sister, who was also a gifted musician. She died of leukemia when she was eight years old, leaving him and his parents devastated. This loss caused him to throw himself even more passionately into his music.

As Joseph told his story, he uncovered a moment in his early teens when he felt the crippling guilt for the first time, the feeling that would so haunt him as an adult. For his birthday, his parents gave him his first grand piano. Prior to this, he had been able to practice on a grand piano only by traveling by bus across town to a music studio. Now he would be able to practice daily, rain or shine.

Joseph's parents arranged to have the piano moved into the living room the night before his birthday, after he had gone to sleep. When he woke in the morning, his parents asked him to close his eyes as they escorted him into the living room. They led him to the piano and asked him to open his eyes. He was seized with joy and gratitude. He hugged his parents and, with tears streaming down his face, sat down at the keyboard. As his fingers were about to touch the keys for the first time, his mother said, "We would never have been able to afford this if your sister hadn't died." Instantly his joy became suffused with guilt and grief. A pattern was set in motion that would play out for the next forty years.

What would cause parents to say such a thing? Unconsciously, they must have wanted him always to remember his sister and be grateful for the too-brief years she had graced their family. Unconsciously, they must have felt deep grief that one child could shine brightly and the other would never do so. The pride they felt in my client would always be accompanied by their grief over the loss of their daughter. They were under the spell of this grief for life, and they unwittingly made sure Joseph would live under it, too.

Fortunately, Joseph was able to break free. He realized that the crime for which he'd been convicted—being alive and thus outshining his sister for all time—was a crime that existed only in his parents' imagination. Many of you may find an issue like this in your past. If so, you will need to ask yourself if you are afraid to go to your ultimate success because you're afraid of outshining someone from long ago. Ask yourself if you're afraid your success will steal attention from someone whom you've been led to believe needs it more.

GOING FORWARD

Now you're equipped with the background knowledge you need for your Big Leap. You understand the basics of the Upper Limit Problem and where its root structure is buried. It's time now to increase the velocity of your learning by going directly into the buzzing intricacy of your life experience. Your Upper Limit Problem lives in the moment-by-moment interactions you have with yourself and the people around you. There is only one way to get this data, and that is to focus your keen awareness on specific aspects of your daily life. In the next chapter I'll show you exactly where to look to find those things. I predict you'll be amazed at the elegant simplicity of the keys to liberation, and doubly amazed that they have been hiding in plain sight.

THREE

Getting Specific

How to Spot the Upper Limit Problem in Daily Life

Now I want to ask you to focus the power of your awareness on several specific actions. The purpose of this exercise is to notice how your particular version of the Upper Limit Problem operates. Once you see it in action, you'll have a new navigational tool for your life. When I was learning to drive, I remember my instructor telling me that driving was more an art than a science. The key to the art, he said, was what he called "benign vigilance," or, paying keen but relaxed attention to what your car and the other cars were doing in every moment. Your journey in the Zone of Genius is just like that. In learning to live in your Zone of Genius, you'll benefit from making a lifelong pursuit out of spotting your Upper Limit behaviors. Make spotting them part of your daily ongoing maintenance procedures, just like brushing your teeth or adjusting the side mirrors of your car.

TYPICAL WAYS WE UPPER-LIMIT OURSELVES

Years ago a client of mine invented a new verb to describe his Upper Limit behavior. He said, "The other day I caught myself in the act of Upper-Limiting myself." It caught on among participants in our seminars, because it puts the Upper Limit Problem in a practical context of something you're *doing*. When you're "Upper-Limiting," you're doing something that is crimping your flow of positive energy. Fortunately, there are not very many ways we Upper-Limit ourselves. Tune in to yourself as you read them, to discover which ones are familiar to you. I'll start with the most common one: worry.

Worry

Worrying is usually a sign that we're Upper-Limiting. It is usually *not* a sign that we're thinking about something useful. The crucial sign that we're worrying unnecessarily is when we're worrying about something we have no control over. Worrying is useful only if it concerns a topic we can actually do something about, and if it leads to our taking positive action right away. All other worry is just Upper Limit noise, designed by our unconscious to keep us safely within our Zone of Excellence or Zone of Competence. Here's how it works:

When things are going well for us, our Upper Limit mechanism kicks in and we suddenly start worrying about things going wrong in some way. We start justifying those worry-thoughts with more worry-thoughts, and soon we are busily manufacturing scenarios of things falling apart, coming unglued, and devolving toward imminent doom.

When I first noticed this tendency in myself, I was amazed at how quickly I could go from a couple of insignificant worry-thoughts to a grandiose doom scenario of the end of civilization. If you notice your worry-thoughts—really study them carefully for a couple of days—you'll find something that may surprise you: almost none of your worry-thoughts have anything to do with reality. Here's what I mean. Let's say you make a cup of coffee in the morning, put it in a to-go cup, and rush off to work. You're speeding along, happily sipping your brew, when suddenly you worry that you may have left the kettle boiling on the stove. That's a reality-based worry-thought. It's worth worrying about, for two reasons: first, your house could burn down; and second, you can do something about it.

There's a good way to know if a worry-thought is something you should pay attention to. Just ask yourself:

Is it a real possibility?

And . . .

Is there any action I can take right now to make a positive difference?

With the kettle, the answers are obviously "Yes" and "Yes." It's a real possibility, and there are positive actions you can take right now. You can go back and check to see if you turned the flame off. You can also call back to the house and have someone else check. However, even these kinds of reality-based worry-thoughts can be an Upper Limit symptom for some people. Some of us worry constantly about whether we've done something wrong or careless like leaving a kettle on. It's a facet of our personality. I know quite a bit about that personality type, having had the opportunity to study an example from the inside for as long as I can remember. It's not important whether you're a born worrier or a newcomer to the habit. All you really need to know is this:

When things are going well, or when you're feeling particularly good, you can always bring yourself down by manufacturing a stream of worry-thoughts. Once you've brought yourself down by worrying, it's very tempting to inflict those worry-thoughts on others. If we're in the grip of worrying while someone around us isn't, we seem to have an almost uncontrollable urge to criticize that person until he or she jumps into the stream of negativity with us.

I once coached a billionaire who worried constantly about losing money. In reality, he could afford to lose a million dollars a day for at least five years and still have a billion left. His worry spilled over into his marriage, into the Upper Limit symptom we'll look at in a moment: blame and criticism. He often bugged his wife because she bought the most expensive brand of toilet paper. She liked a particular kind, but he was always trying to convince her that cheaper alternatives were just as good. In a situation like that, it's pretty clear that tissue's not the real issue.

It took a bit of gentle pummeling on my part before he finally he saw that his worry and criticism were just ways of disrupting the flow of positive energy in his life and in the relationship. Since he was a guy who lived by the numbers, I started by asking him to get out a calculator and figure the actual costs of the toilet paper. I said, "Imagine she went on a wild binge and started buying a hundred rolls every day! And imagine if she really went off the deep end and bought a hundred rolls a day for the next fifty years. How much would she have spent fifty years from now, when you're both ninety years old?" He punched in numbers and came up with the cost of her lifelong extravaganza: $1.5 million. I then asked him to calculate what percentage of his net worth it amounted to. He didn't even have to use the calculator for that part of the assignment. I don't remember the exact number, but it was far less than 1 percent. I asked him how much his net worth varied from day to day due to ordinary stock-market fluctuations. He said that it would sometimes vary by as much as a hundred million dollars from hour to hour. I pointed out that even if his wife went on a superbinge and bought a thousand rolls a day, it still wouldn't amount to a single day's fluctuation. "Given that," I said, "what's the real reason you're criticizing your wife?"

There's a saying I've developed, based on many counseling sessions that revolved around money struggles: money arguments never have anything to do with money. Money arguments are always about something deeper, and it was certainly true in his case. We discovered that deep down he didn't feel that he deserved to be wealthy *and* loved, too. He had grown up in a wealthy family, but according to him, his parents spent much of every day in a pitched battle with each other. Without realizing it, he was carrying on in his own marriage the family tradition of constant bickering. In his original family, the formula was "money equals arguing." It didn't matter if the amount was a hundred million dollars or a few bucks for good toilet paper; if there was money involved, there had to be an argument about it.

I gave him the assignment of going cold turkey with criticism and blame. I asked him to call a complete halt to criticizing his wife about money. To engage his competitive powers, I told him I highly doubted he could stop criticizing his wife about money for even one day. Jutting his jaw defiantly, he took up the challenge. When he and his wife came in for their next session, they both looked about ten years younger. They had even taken his assignment to a higher level, both of them deciding to eliminate criticism in general from their relationship. He told me that they had spent a delightful week "celebrating what we have rather than carping about what we don't have."

I encourage you to make a careful study of your worry habits. I've seen a lot of lives change, including my own, when people drop their addiction to worry. And yes, worry is definitely an addiction. In fact, worrying is like playing a slot machine in a gambling casino. Occasionally the worrier will hit the jackpot and be rewarded for something that actually happens. If you worry long enough about the stock market crashing, you'll eventually hit the jackpot, because from time to time it's always going to crash.

Being a recovering worrywart myself, I know a lot about chronic worriers. I didn't realize until I was nearly thirty that most of my worrying was about things I had absolutely no control over. Up until then I thought worrying was somehow helpful and useful. In fact, I believed that if everybody else wasn't as worried as I was about the things I worried about, there was clearly something wrong with them. Gradually I came to see that I was just worrying for the sake of choking the flow of positive energy in myself. Worrying was one way I was Upper-Limiting myself.

Did you ever see the great Woody Allen movie *Annie Hall*? There's an illuminating scene in it that shows how the Upper Limit Problem works in relationships. Woody is running frantically around the bedroom, wringing his hands and trying to get his wife interested in his latest conspiracy theory about the Kennedy assassination. She looks on with patient exasperation until finally his rant slows down enough for her to get a word in edgewise. She gently suggests that maybe these obsessions of his are simply ways of avoiding intimacy with her. There's a long pause while he considers her point. The audience anticipates that he will mount an outraged denial. Finally he says, "You're right."

There is a lot of wisdom in that moment of inspired cinema. If you took a random look inside any person's mind, chances are you'd find some worrying going on. If you suggest to the person that those worry-thoughts are simply ways to avoid feeling the flow of positive energy, chances are the person won't say, "You're right." They'll probably argue that their worrying is absolutely essential to the correct functioning of the universe and that if they stopped worrying the whole enterprise would collapse. I know, because I used to feel that way myself. I thought my twenty-four-hour-a-day stream of worry-thoughts was the correct response to life. It took me a long time to figure out that 99 percent of my worrying was completely unnecessary. It was very humbling to realize that my worries were there just to make me miserable. It was even more humbling to realize that I was the guy who had his finger firmly pressed on the misery button. It was wonderful, though, to discover that I also had the power to quit pressing the button.

Worry: What You Can Do Right Now

Now I make it a daily practice to spot my worry-thoughts. If you do that, you can use them as springboards into your Zone of Genius. I'd like to show you the tool I've developed. It's a sequence of moves that will reliably get you out of the worry trap. Let me take you through the moves step-by-step and then follow with a real-life example.

1. I notice myself worrying about something.

2. I let go of the worry-thoughts, shifting my focus away from them.

3. I wonder: what positive new thing is trying to come into being?

4. I usually get a body feeling (not a thought or idea) of where that positive new thing is trying to come through.

5. I open my focus to feel that body feeling deeply.

6. I let myself feel it deeply for as long as I possibly can.

7. Later, I often get an idea of the positive thing that was trying to come through.

Here's a walk-through of the process, using a real example.

1. I'm walking down the street of my town on a Saturday afternoon. I pass a jewelry store where my wife, Kathlyn, and I have bought beautiful pieces over the years. I glance in the window as I pass, admiring some

of the items. About fifteen seconds later I notice some worry-thoughts about money. Specifically, the worry-thoughts are about whether we have enough money to help a gifted young member of our family go to the private music conservatory she wants to attend.

2. I notice the worry-thoughts and let them go, just dropping them in mid-thought without pursuing them.

3. I wonder what positive thing is trying to come through.

4. I feel a pleasant sensation in my throat.

5. As I walk along, I let myself feel it thoroughly, savoring the pleasant sensation.

6. A few minutes later, getting into my car, the insight occurs to me that seeing the jewelry in the window triggered a wave of guilt about the level of abundance my wife and I enjoy, compared with other members of our extended family. Seeing the jewelry also sparked a feeling inside me of how much I love and appreciate my wife, and how I wish there was some piece of jewelry that could really express the depth of those feelings. I sit in my car for a few moments before turning on the engine, letting myself enjoy the sweet feelings of how much I love and appreciate

my wife, and how much I appreciate the prosperity we've created in our lives. I realize there's no physical object like jewelry that could express those feelings. They exist in the nonmaterial world, in the feeling of flowing connection between us.

7. I pick up my phone and call Kathlyn. She's out doing errands, too, and it turns out she's about two blocks away from where I'm sitting in my car. I tell her the sequence I just experienced, from the glance in the window to the worry-thoughts to the delicious moment of letting myself feel the overflow of love and appreciation for her. I say, "Let's make sure we take more time to celebrate what we have."

8. She agrees and gives me a big virtual kiss. I say good-bye, start my car, and head home.

Let's explore what happened here. First of all, I chose not to regard my worry-thoughts about money as being actually about money. That's the attitude I want you to take toward your worry-thoughts in general. I want you to see them as Upper Limit symptoms, unless they are about something real that you can do something about right away. In my case, I was walking down a street on an errand run when I had the worry-thoughts about whether we had enough money to send the member of my extended family to music school. My mind quickly computed that those thoughts were not about something real. In reality I can easily afford to help my niece out. The real issue is not money. It's whether I want to deal with the emotional dynamics that often accompany giving money to a family member. In addition, the worry-thoughts were not about something I needed to act on right away. Even if I wanted to provide the money, I was not likely to stop on the street and make a phone call to transfer funds. That was a second reason my mind computed that these worry-thoughts were more likely an Upper Limit Problem.

This computation only took a nanosecond. That's what I'd like you to aim for, too. With practice you'll get very nimble at noticing which thoughts are ones you should pay attention to and which ones you can dismiss. Speaking of dismissing, I'd like you to notice how I simply dropped the chain of thoughts about money. Imagine squeezing a tennis ball in your hand, then releasing your grip and dropping the ball. A lot of people don't realize that they can dismiss worry-thoughts just like that. One moment the thoughts have a grip on you; then you suddenly realize it's you who have the grip on them. You release the grip, and the thoughts disappear. They come back again, and you release them again. With practice, they disappear and don't come back, if you give your mind a more productive thing to do. The productive thing to do is to look for the positive new emergence that's trying to happen. In other words, when you find yourself worrying, know that there is something positive trying to break through. Your worry-thoughts, particularly if you find yourself recycling the same ones over and over, are a flag waving at you from your Zone of Genius. Something is trying to get your attention. Look beyond the worry-thoughts, and you will often find a new direction that's being laid out for you.

When I'm operating in my Zone of Genius, I am doing what I love to do and I'm enjoying what I have. My worry-thoughts about money were simply a sign. The sign said it's time for me to expand my capacity to revel in the joy of having created abundance *and* love. To my knowledge, that combination is something new in my family lineage. It's new territory, and I'm learning to live in it. To do that, I need to overcome thousands of years of programming that adversity is a constant requirement of existence. We need to savor our success, first for seconds at a time, then for minutes that grow into months.

It's a heroic task. Science tells us that it took a very long time for our fish ancestors to evolve the necessary equipment to turn those initial flops on dry land into walks. Now we're in a stage of evolution in which we're doing the inner equivalent of those early fish flops: we're learning to let ourselves enjoy love, abundance, and other forms of positive energy without sabotaging ourselves. Patience is called for, along with a good pat on the back for ourselves when we have moments of savoring our good fortune.

Criticism and Blame

I mentioned earlier that most worry-thoughts have absolutely nothing to do with reality. That's true for criticism, too. In other words, when we criticize something, it usually doesn't have anything to do with the thing we're criticizing. When we blame someone or something, we're doing it because we've hit our Upper Limit and are trying to retard the flow of positive energy.

When this fact first dawned on me, I had trouble accepting it. I had spent years perfecting my criticize-and-blame mechanism. When I was in the act of criticizing or blaming, I was completely convinced that the other person had done something that needed criticizing. Criticizing and blaming are like being in a hypnotic trance. When we're in the trance, we really believe that the other person has done wrong. You've probably seen the kind of stage hypnotism where the hypnotist gets the subject to believe he's a dog or a chicken. The subject barks on command or struts about the stage flapping imaginary wings. The audience roars with delight, probably because we recognize that we spend a good bit of our own lives in a trance.

Criticism and blame are addictions. They are costly addictions, because they are the number-one destroyer of intimacy in close relationships. When people give the reasons for breaking up with someone, the most common one goes something like this: "I got tired of the constant criticism and blame." With that in mind, it becomes doubly important to regard criticism and blame as addictions.

If you want to find out if your Upper Limit behavior is an addiction, here's a quick experiment: Try to stop it for a day and see what happens. If it's not an addiction, you'll be able to stop right away. If it's an addiction, it will creep back into your behavior unconsciously, just as smokers who quit find a cigarette back in their hands without even realizing it.

Self-criticism and criticizing others are one and the same. In other words, self-blame is part of the same Upper Limit pattern as blaming someone else. Both criticizing yourself and criticizing others are highly addictive and very popular ways of busting up the flow of positive energy. Remember earlier when I said that worry is useful only if it concerns something real that you can do something about? Criticism works the same way. It is useful only if it's directed at a specific thing and produces a useful result. For example, if I'm standing on your toe in an elevator, go ahead and criticize me. It's useful, especially if it produces the result of liberating your toe from the tyranny of my shoe.

Chronic criticism and *chronic blame* are the behaviors we really need to eliminate. They are never about producing a result. I coached John, a top executive at Dell Computer, some years ago about a problem that was causing considerable stress in his work group. The problem was that he would sometimes explode in anger and blast off a stream of criticism at someone or the entire group. On some occasions John would even go so far as to beat on the table with his fist and turn beet red in the face. This behavior wasn't so much a problem for him as it was for the others. Ten seconds after the explosion, he would forget about it. "Don't pay any attention to it," he'd say. "I don't mean anything by it, and I never hold grudges." Unfortunately, the recipients of his wrath were not blessed with the "just forget about it" mechanism. Some of them would still be smarting from his explosions days or even weeks later.

Why was this pattern an Upper Limit behavior? When I worked it through with John, we discovered that these blow-ups often followed on the heels of some good news. For example, one of his executives would do something noteworthy. My client would start to feel a positive flow of energy and would have the urge to give the person a compliment. Then his Upper Limit would kick in, and he would start thinking of ways the person had disappointed him in the past. The disappointment would curdle quickly into anger, and a blow-up would ensue. When I asked around among the executives, none of them could ever remember John giving them a compliment.

John made a commitment to ending the pattern of anger explosions. We went to work on breaking up the problematic sequence. I had him role-play giving a compliment to one of the executives, using myself as the stand-in. When he opened his mouth to give the compliment, John started coughing furiously. I invited him to pause and tune in to the feelings that were behind the coughing. He reported that it reminded him of his father, fifty years before, giving him compliments that were really criticisms, such as "You're finally getting the grades you should have been getting all along." John told me he ultimately learned to cringe anytime his father said something positive to him, because he knew it was going to have a backhand slap concealed in it. "I never knew when the ax was going to fall," he said.

I gently pointed out that he was perpetuating the same pattern with his executives. Many of them had told me that they often avoided going to him with important issues because they never knew when one of his blow-ups was going to happen. John slumped back in his chair when this insight sank in. He sat there for a moment, seemingly stunned, and then said, "I want to fix that." As soon as he left the meeting with me, John called his executives together and told them what he'd just learned. I chose not to participate in the meeting, lest it seem that I was masterminding his revelations. Later I heard from my client and the executives that it had been one of the most powerful moments of their business careers. The executives were particularly moved to see a powerful person they admired be so genuine with them.

My assignment to you: become a keen observer of critical statements that come out of your mouth or fly through your mind. Begin to sort them into two piles: Pile One contains all the criticisms about real things you plan to do something about ("Hey, you're standing on my toe. Get off!"); Pile Two contains all the others. I predict you'll make the humbling but liberating discovery, as I did, that Pile Two towers over the paltry stack in Pile One.

Deflecting

Many of us crimp the flow of positive energy by avoiding it altogether. The mechanism we use is what I call *deflection;* it's so common we almost take it for granted in human life. Think of how many times you've heard conversations like the following example of deflection:

JOE: You did a great job on that presentation.
JACK: Nah, I ran out of time and had to leave out some of the best stuff.
JOE: Still, I noticed that people were really paying attention.
JACK: I'm glad they weren't paying too close attention, because they would have seen more places I messed up.

Deflection keeps the positive energy from landing, being received, and being acknowledged. Notice how simple and gracious it would be if Jack handled the moment in a different way: by receiving and acknowledging the positive energy instead of deflecting it:

JOE: You did a great job on that presentation.

JACK: Thanks. I appreciate you for saying that. I'm glad it came across well, because I felt bad about running out of time and leaving out some of the best stuff.

Here, Jack received the appreciation instead of flicking it off. He acknowledged Joe for the expression of positive energy, adding his own reservations about the presentation only after he let the appreciation land on him.

When we shut out positive energy through deflection, we keep ourselves safely in our Zone of Competence or Zone of Excellence. Deflection keeps us from challenging ourselves, preventing us from expanding our capacity for experiencing positive energy.

If you want to study deflection up close, spend a little time on a golf course. Golfers seem particularly skilled at deflecting positive energy. (By the way, lest anyone think I'm a golf whiz, I'm a seventeen handicapper who employs perseverance and enthusiasm to overcome a remarkable lack of natural athletic skill.)

A while back the CEO of a Fortune 500 company was visiting me to get some coaching in handling a boardroom relationship issue. Ed was an avid golfer, and since my home office is right next to one of the best golf courses on the West Coast, our afternoon coaching session spilled over into a late-afternoon round. As fate would have it, we were paired with two attorneys, whom I'll call Al and Bob, up from Beverly Hills for a day of golf. My client and I had been working on his Upper Limit Problem all day long, and I could not have asked for a better example of deflection than our two golf-mates provided. Throughout the round they engaged in one deflection after another. Here are a few examples:

Me: Nice shot, Al.

Al: Nah, I didn't make full contact.

Ed (my client): Beautiful putt, Bob!

Bob: It's about time I got one in. My putting has been horrible all day.

Me: Wow, great approach shot, Bob! (He'd just hit his pitching wedge from a hundred yards out to land three feet from the hole.)

Bob: Yeah, well, I got lucky that time. Even a blind squirrel gets an acorn now and then.

On and on it went. They were both excellent golfers, but to hear their dialogue, you would have thought they were the worst of hackers. It was a perfect addition to my coaching day with Ed, because we got to study deflection with a couple of masters. By the time the round was over, my client had seen so many deflections that I doubt he ever uttered another one in his life.

Here's what to do when you notice yourself deflecting. When someone says the equivalent of "Nice shot" to you, pause for a moment to register the beam of positive energy that's being aimed at you. Then thank the person who beamed it your way. For example, when I said, "Nice shot, Al," he could just as easily have let my positive comment register on him. He could have taken a moment to feel pleasure in the shot, and he could have thanked me for the expression of positive energy I beamed in his direction. The dialogue would have gone like this:

ME: Nice shot, Al.
AL: Thank you. I wish I'd made better contact with it, but it came out pretty good anyway.

The art of getting beyond our Upper Limit Problem has a lot to do with creating space within us to feel and appreciate natural good feelings. By *natural* I mean good feelings that aren't induced by alcohol, sugar, and other short-term fixes. Letting yourself savor natural good feelings is a direct way to transcend your Upper Limit Problem. By extending your ability to feel positive feelings, you expand your tolerance for things going well in your life.

In golf, there are plenty of natural good feelings to enjoy. There's the beauty of the course, the satisfaction of a ball well struck, the fellowship of a good walk with companions. These are ideal conditions for triggering an Upper Limit Problem. There's another reason golf makes a perfect place to explore the Upper Limit Problem: the ball doesn't move until you hit it. In other sports you can attribute your lack of success to the skill of your opponent. You struck out because the pitcher had "a wicked curve" or the wide receiver outsprinted you. Golfers have no such luxury. The little ball just sits there until you make it go somewhere else. In that regard, golf is very much like life itself, which awaits your intention and action before revealing the mysteries of the outcome.

Squabbling

Arguments are one of the most common ways of bringing yourself down when you've hit your Upper Limit. When things are going well, you can crimp the flow of positive energy quickly by starting a conflict. Then, the conflict develops a life of its own, lasting for hours, days, or even years. The net effect: you drop back into your Zone of Competence or your Zone of Excellence. Genius takes a backseat.

If you can learn to see arguments as Upper Limit symptoms, you can make big breakthroughs in getting beyond them. There is tremendous practical value in making this move. For example, once Kathlyn and I figured out that our arguments were Upper Limit symptoms, we were able to reduce drastically the number of conflicts we had. As of this writing, we haven't had an argument in more than twelve years. We rechanneled all that wasted argument energy into creative energy, writing four books together and giving several hundred presentations together during those twelve years. (Sometimes when we mention this point in lectures, an audience member will raise a hand and ask, "Isn't it boring if you don't argue?" That's kind of like asking, "Isn't peace boring? Don't human beings need wars to spice things up?" We can definitely testify that having a great time creating things together is anything but boring.)

First, understand why arguments occur. Arguments are caused by two people (or two countries) racing to occupy the victim position in the relationship. Person A claims the victim position ("Why are you doing this to me?") and then tries to get person B to agree with that assessment. In other words, person B has to agree that he or she is the persecutor. Therein lies the problem. It's almost impossible to get the other guy to agree that it's his fault. In nearly five thousand sessions of assisting people in resolving conflicts, I have never, ever witnessed the following kind of interchange:

PERSON A: Why are you making me so miserable? This problem is entirely your fault.

PERSON B: Wow, thanks for pointing that out. I agree completely. It's clear that I'm the perpetrator, you're the victim, and your misery is entirely my fault.

However, I *have* seen about five thousand variations on the following:

PERSON A: Why are you making me so miserable? This problem is entirely your fault.

PERSON B: I'm making *you* miserable? *I'm* the one who's the victim here. It's your fault, not mine. I've been putting up with your guff so long I ought to get some sort of martyrdom prize!

PERSON A: That's absurd. Let me tell you all the reasons *I'm* the real victim here.

PERSON B: Great. Then when you get through, I'll tell you how all of them are your fault, always have been, and always will be.

Once the race for the victim position is under way, each person must find some way to out-victim the other. In other words, each person must present an escalating series of "proofs" that he or she is the real victim. In conflicts around the house, violence does not usually ensue, but in conflicts between countries or ethnic or religious groups, violence often erupts during the process. During the Bosnian conflict in the nineties, I was facilitating a seminar in which some Bosnians were taking part. One of them said, "Nobody can really understand the conflict unless you realize it's been going on since 1389." Most of the participants laughed, thinking he was making a joke. He wasn't joking, though, and went on to explain that the two factions have been in conflict for more than six hundred years. Since they all have the same skin color and speak the same languages, the only thing separating the two sides is a difference in beliefs and centuries of claiming victimhood.

Once two sides start jockeying for the victim position, the race can stretch into generations. Once it gets under way between countries or between religious or ethnic groups, it can go on for centuries.

Understanding the physics of arguments will reveal how conflicts—whether between a couple, board members, countries, or religious groups—can be resolved. In fact, it's the only way I've ever found that will resolve conflicts permanently. The key insight: each entity in a situation represents 100 percent. Each entity in a conflict has 100 percent of the responsibility for resolving the conflict. In other words, person A is a whole and complete 100 percent, and person B is a whole and complete 100 percent. If two people are involved, there is 200 percent responsibility to be divided up. The fatal mistake is thinking that there is 100 percent of responsibility to be divided up; this approach requires each person to take some portion of the 100 percent. It's a massive thinking error that causes massive problems, because it leads to endless jockeying for the victim position.

If you don't realize that each person is a 100 percent entity, you're left with the impossible task of apportioning 100 percent among the participants in the conflict. This can take on absurd qualities, as was evidenced by a malpractice suit in Denver some years ago in which the jury found the doctor 82 percent responsible and the patient 18 percent responsible. How they came up with this number remains a mystery, but even the judge marveled at the absurdity of it. Once you start trying to apportion 100 percent among two or more people, you enter a surreal tunnel from which there is only one escape. The only way out is to assign each party 100 percent, and to invite each party to take it.

If both people will claim 100 percent responsibility, there's a possibility of ending the conflict. Nothing less than 100 percent will work. Since there's 200 percent responsibility to be shared, jockeying for the victim position means that you're demanding that the other person take more than 100 percent while you take less than 100 percent. Nobody in his right mind would agree to a deal like that, and it's pretty clear that trying to negotiate these kinds of deals has been a total flop over the past few thousand years.

How would this approach play out in a real-life conflict such as that in the Middle East? It boils down to something very simple:

Muslims: No matter what's happened in the past, we now take 100 percent responsibility for creating this conflict and 100 percent responsibility for resolving it.

Jews: No matter what's happened in the past, we now take 100 percent responsibility for creating this conflict and 100 percent responsibility for resolving it.

Many people will look at that simple solution and say, "That's impossible!" However, if you told a visitor from another planet that some earthlings had been squabbling about the same thing for several thousand years, the visitor would probably say, "That's impossible!" It's no more impossible, then, to create a new way of dealing with conflicts, through both sides in every conflict taking 100 percent responsibility.

Let's start at home, though—in our bedrooms and board-rooms. From the experience of hundreds of sessions, I can tell you that this method of problem resolution works wonders. When people step out of the victim position and take 100 per-cent responsibility, their marriages and their businesses flour-ish. The moment is always exquisite to behold. If you would like to behold some of these exquisite moments yourself, please watch the video examples at the Big Leap Web site.

Let's do it a new way for the next few thousand years.

Getting Sick, Getting Hurt

When things are going well, some of us have a pattern that is pure Upper Limit Problem: we get sick or get hurt. To find out whether some of your ills or accidents are due to the Upper Limit Problem, take a moment to think back over times when you've gotten sick or gotten hurt in an accident. You probably won't be able to remember very many of them in detail; mer-cifully, our minds filter out the excruciating details of many of life's unpleasant incidents. If you can pull up memories of some of your illnesses and accidents, ask yourself if they came during or just after a big win in business or a period of good times in a relationship.

Not all illnesses or accidents are Upper Limit symptoms, of course. A skeptic might ask, "Hey, can't I just get sick because I get sneezed on? Can't I just fall off my bike sometimes? Does it always have to be an Upper Limit Problem?" The answer: people get sick for all sorts of reasons. However, if you are keenly interested in taking your Big Leap, you will want to examine everything that brings you pain and suffering as a potential Upper Limit symptom. You may find that you can be a lot healthier than you ever imagined.

So many of us simply never look at the effect of our minds and emotions on our physical health. But the payoff for doing so is well worth it. Once I caught on to how my Upper Limit Problem was affecting me, I began to examine every aspect of my life. For example, if I felt the sniffles and scratchy throat of a cold coming on, I would pause to wonder whether I was Upper-Limiting myself. I soon discovered that I could ward off colds if I regarded them as Upper Limit symptoms. It made a huge difference in my health. As of this writing I haven't had a cold or flu in thirteen years. A lot of the credit for that long-running streak of health must go to my thinking of getting sick and getting hurt as Upper Limit symptoms. Let me explain in more detail about exactly how to do this for yourself.

THE THREE *P*S

Your exploration will go easier if you have a map. The map I use is what I call the Three *P*s: punishment, prevention, and protection. The Three *P*s can help you understand the real driving force behind many illnesses and accidents. I've probably got a few hundred examples of each of these in my files; let me use a few vivid ones to illustrate the Three *P*s.

- *Punishment.* Ryan, a successful middle-aged stockbroker, married and a pillar of the community, starts to suffer from what he calls "killer migraines." When I explore it with him, I discover that he often gets them in the midafternoon. When I explore it further, he lets his hair down and confesses: on the occasions he gets the midafternoon migraines, he has usually spent his lunch hour having irrational, exuberant sex with his young secretary. Ryan has not mentioned these wild romps to his wife.

It turns out to be a classic example of the first *P*, punishment. It's not hard to see why he might be punishing himself with his "killer" migraines. He gets it right away when I explain the Upper Limit Problem to him. He tells me that he is having more fun than he's had in ages. Intellectually, he knows that cheating and lying are not only endangering his career but also destroying the intimacy in his marriage. However, the ecstatic sex doesn't just feel good; it's giving him what feels like a midlife rebirth. He's once again feeling the reckless passion of his motorcycle-riding youth.

If his rational, sober, conscious mind were in charge, Ryan might come up with a noble solution such as this:

These delicious feelings have nothing to do with my secretary. I'm using my affair with her to awaken feelings I've been submerging for years under my dutiful life and comfortable marriage. This affair is showing me that I am failing to be my best and settling to live beneath my Zone of Genius. My affair is an Upper Limit Problem. I'm going to make a sincere commitment to living in my Zone of Genius, so I can feel ecstatically alive all the time without lying and cheating to get there!

That's how his rational, sober conscious mind might handle it. However, our unconscious minds are not rational and sober; they're direct and to the point. His unconscious mind's solution is to punish him with a killer migraine for feeling so much ecstasy. The migraine is a tool of his Upper Limit Problem, and it speaks in a blunt language he cannot ignore. It quickly brings him back to earth after his lunchtime excursions into the stratosphere. The headache is literally a killjoy, saying, "Welcome back to the painful consequences of lying, cheating, and not heeding the call to live in your Zone of Genius."

Ryan didn't get to be a top executive by being a slow learner, so it didn't take him long to handle the situation. He said a painful good-bye to the lunchtime trysts and had a considerably more painful series of conversations with his wife. Ryan got one immediate reward for these courageous conversations: the migraines stopped. Many physical symptoms such as headache and back pain are warning signs, like the flapping and wobble of a flat tire when you're driving on the highway. The symptoms are saying, *Slow down, stop what you're doing, and pay attention, because there's something out of integrity here.*

Fortunately Ryan got the message in time to wake up and handle the situation. He had two big tasks ahead of him: rebuilding his marriage, and building a new home in his Zone of Genius. It took him the better part of the next two years to do both those things. He had to say no to a lot of his former activities and yes to dreams and visions that had been simmering within him for years. For one thing, he and his wife both realized that the enormous home they lived in no longer suited them now that their children were grown. For another, he shifted his focus within his company to mentoring younger executives rather than front-line management. Mentoring was in his Zone of Genius. He thrived on it, and it provided major benefits to the company.

- I link together the other two *Ps—prevention* and *protection*—because they almost always occur at the same time. Here's the bottom line on prevention and protection: when you suffer symptoms of illness or experience an accident, you often do so because you're unconsciously trying to prevent yourself from having to do something you don't really want to do and/or protect yourself from something you don't want to feel. The illness or accident is your unconscious mind's clunky way of doing you a favor. It's a costly favor, though, and once you learn how to navigate your Upper Limits, you can move through your barriers in a much more friendly way than making yourself sick or having an accident. Having created a few unnecessary illnesses and accidents myself, I can testify that acting consciously is better.

Let me give you an example of how prevention and protection work. Years ago when I was a university professor, I shared an office for a while with a brilliant colleague named Dr. Smith. Every month, one of us made a presentation on our work to the other faculty members. In these presentations, we described our current activities and talked about where we were going with our work over the next year. There were about a dozen professors in my department, so the opportunity to make a presentation came around only once a year. On the morning of Dr. Smith's presentation, he showed up with laryngitis. I got to the office a half hour before his presentation only to find him croaking to the dean that he wouldn't be able to do it. After the dean departed to cancel the meeting, I expressed my sympathies and remarked that I couldn't recall his ever missing a lecture due to illness. In fact, he had the reputation of being an "iron man" in the sense of never missing a class. I asked him if he might be willing to explore his laryngitis as an Upper Limit symptom. As you might recall, my breakthrough theory happened at Stanford, and this was one of my first opportunities to test it. Dr. Smith said he would, and in our conversation we uncovered a classic example of prevention and protection.

He told me that he and his wife had spent a wonderful weekend celebrating a decision he'd finally made. For a long time Dr. Smith had wanted to break out of his university job and work in the private sector. An opportunity had opened up in a neighboring state, and he had gone there for the interview the previous Friday. Over the weekend he had decided to take the job, and "Saturday night we broke out a bottle of great champagne we'd been saving for a special occasion." As Monday loomed, though, Dr. Smith had to face sober reality again. He didn't want to tell the university yet, because there were still some key details to work out about the new position. You can probably appreciate the bind he was in. Dr. Smith was happier and more excited than he had been in a long time, but he didn't want to talk about it yet. Instead, in his presentation he had to appear enthusiastic about research he didn't want to be doing at a university where he no longer wanted to work. He didn't relish the idea of lying and faking it, but he couldn't figure out how to handle the situation any other way. This is the kind of double bind that freezes up the conscious mind's rational thought processes. It's in these moments that the unconscious mind goes to work on a solution. The solutions it comes up with are often inelegant and primitive, but they are direct and effective (and usually involve pain of some kind).

The solution Dr. Smith's unconscious mind came up with was laryngitis. Prevention and protection came to the rescue.

His croaky voice prevented him from having to give the presentation and protected him from the embarrassment of being a phony. An illness with prominent, audible symptoms like laryngitis is a socially acceptable way of getting out of almost any activity.

Halfway through our conversation, the laryngitis disappeared and his voice returned to normal (although he didn't notice it at first). Like a ringing telephone, many symptoms—even the most painful ones—stop annoying you when you get the message. He had a jaw-dropping moment of surprise when he finally realized he was speaking normally. It would probably make a better story if I told you he dashed into the dean's office, blurted out his guilty truths, and proceeded with his presentation. What actually happened, though, was that he chose to keep his mouth shut and head back home to restore the celebratory mood with his wife.

The next time you find yourself with a stomachache, a throbbing head, or a stubbed toe, ask yourself if you might be Upper-Limiting. Sometimes a headache's just a headache, but often if you look a little deeper you'll find that it's an expression of your Upper Limit Problem. Then, it's a signal that you need to expand instead of contract. It's telling you that it's time to open up and embrace a new high-water mark of positive energy that's trying to establish itself in you. Underneath the headache might be an insight that is as powerfully positive as the pain is negative. The surface pain is often caused by resisting the underlying positive message. Sometimes the positive message is a message we're afraid to hear, such as "It's time to quit my job and do something else." I've sat with dozens of clients as they made this kind of discovery, realizing that they had unconsciously preferred dealing with the pain of the chronic headache or back pain rather than the fear and uncertainty of the underlying message. The bad news is that pain can last a long time if we're unwilling to pay attention to the hidden message. The good news is that the fear and uncertainty last only as long as it takes us to hear the underlying positive message and begin to act on it.

INTEGRITY BREACH

Committing a breach of integrity is one of the quickest ways to bring yourself down after an excursion past your Upper Limit. The most popular integrity breaches are lies, broken agreements, and withheld truths. If you will begin to focus your keen awareness on those three behaviors, you can make huge strides in transcending your Upper Limit and establishing yourself in your Zone of Genius.

Begin by understanding integrity on the most practical level of daily reality. Many people think of integrity as a moral issue, and of course in part it is. However, there's a much more fundamental way to think of integrity. If you think of integrity as a physics issue instead of a moral one, you'll see that it belongs alongside unarguable forces such as gravity. Long before morality came into play, the original definition of integrity had to do with wholeness and completeness. To be in integrity meant you were whole and complete. To be out of integrity meant a breach in your wholeness had occurred; there was a gap in your completeness. Thinking of integrity as a physics issue gives you a much more practical tool than regarding it simply as a moral issue. Morality is about good and bad, right and wrong—all of which are highly arguable. Physics is about did and didn't, not is and isn't. Let me give an example of how a physics approach to integrity can be valuable in daily life.

Think of communication between people as a flow of energy. Think of your communication with your own inner depths in the same way. A breach of integrity stops the flow of energy, just as a pebble jammed in a garden hose stops the flow of water. Let's say you and I meet on the street. "How're you doing?" you ask. "Fine," I say. You notice, though, that I look anything but fine. You notice that my mouth is downturned in a slight grimace and that a vertical worry-furrow is etched in my brow. Now you have a choice. You can do the "polite" thing and overlook what you see. Or you can make mention of what you noticed by going to a deeper level of communication: "Are you really fine? You look worried about something." (By the way, I recommend that you break the surface like this only with people you care about. I don't think it's worth your while to go to this deeper level with the pizza delivery guy or the meter maid.)

If you decide to break through the surface politeness by calling attention to my worried brow, you keep the flow of communication going between us. If you don't, the flow stops. Here's why. The flow of communication includes your awareness of my furrowed brow. If you choose not to mention this awareness, the flow gets blocked. Pressure builds up as the flow looks for how to make a detour around the blockage. It's a pebble in the hose. I'm not saying it's a bad pebble; that would be the moral approach to the problem. It's just a force to be reckoned with. It's a gap in the completeness of the communication between us.

Consider the moment Bill Clinton uttered those magic words "I did not have sexual relations with that woman." I happened to be watching that moment on television, and I groaned when he said it. My wife and I (both of whom had voted for him) turned to look at each other with raised eyebrows, because we knew immediately that he was lying. How did we know that? Go watch the moment yourself (it's on YouTube.com and other such sites), and you'll see what tipped us off. When he speaks those words, he makes a little head jiggle and sideways cut with his eyes. I'd seen the same little expression dozens of times in therapy sessions with juvenile delinquents and others when they were trying to lie. In poker terms it's a "tell." In body-language research, it's a clue to deception. To us, it was flashing neon sign that said a lot more than "I actually *did* have sex with that woman." It was also saying, "I'm a naughty little boy who'll keep acting out until I get caught."

People of Clinton's personality type are compelled to keep testing the limits. They're unconsciously trying to find out whether they can outsmart everybody else, and they keep escalating until they discover the situation where they can't. Why? When one of John F. Kennedy's friends asked him why he would risk getting caught and compromising national security by sneaking lovers into the White House, he said, "I can't help it." "I can't help it" is not an attractive quality to have in a president, but the general public never had to come face-to-face with it as we did with Clinton. Kennedy served a shorter time in office and enjoyed a less inquisitive press corps used to keeping mum about such things.

Clinton's saga is pure Upper Limit Problem. Elected president twice, he was riding a wave of high approval ratings and a booming economy with, of all things, a budget surplus in the offing. A tiny voice somewhere in him whispered, "Things can't possibly be this good." His Upper Limit switch tripped, and history had its way with him.

Like most people, I think that lying is morally wrong, but for a moment just think of Clinton's fib as a physics issue. The lie jammed a pebble in the garden hose. The flow was impeded; it took fifty million dollars and a year of everybody's time to dislodge the pebble. As more details emerged, the war between the pebble and the flow got bigger and bigger until the inevitable happened. The DNA on Lewinsky's famous blue dress finally got him. (Note to future presidents who are tempted to tell whopper lies: the flow always wins. For irrefutable evidence, have a look at the Grand Canyon.)

Now let's shift the focus to the practical realities of daily life. Most of us will not encounter Upper Limit Problems that require DNA analysis, impeachment, and other Clinton-sized phenomena. So, where are we likely to find our integrity breaches? The first place to look is in the subtle ways we lie to ourselves in order to conceal feelings we do not want to accept consciously. Let me give you an example. I worked with Sarah and Jonah, a married couple who shared the leadership of a family business that had grown rapidly to forty million dollars in annual revenues. In our first session they traded complaints about various things; the one that had "really got his goat," he said, was when she accused him of sexual flirtations with two of the employees. He had hotly denied having sexual feelings for either of the women, and the issue had quickly escalated into the same squabble that had been going on for months. One of the hazards of family businesses is that squabbles spread through the nonfamily employees faster than the family usually realizes. The couple had finally decided to come see me when a key employee took them aside one day and said, "I don't know what's going on between you two, but can you please fix it as soon as possible? It's driving the rest of us nuts."

I called a time-out and asked Sarah and Jonah when this cycle of arguing had first come up. Their answer confirmed my suspicion that it was an Upper Limit Problem: the squabble had erupted on the heels of their best-ever quarterly earnings report. They had not noticed that their squabble had broken out right after a celebration. An Upper Limit Problem puts people into an altered state of consciousness. We "go unconscious" in the sense of losing touch with our rational faculties. We don't see the bigger picture.

I asked Sarah and Jonah a specific question designed to wake them up from the trance of their argument:

Would you be willing to consider that your conflict is not about what you think it's about?

Early in my work on transcending my own Upper Limit, I made a key discovery: if I could consider, even for a moment, that I was not upset for the reason I thought I was, I could break out of the trance I was in. Then, I could begin to see what the real issues were. When awakened from a trance, though, many of us come to with a startled *Huh?* That's how my clients responded, so I gave them a quick explanation of how the Upper Limit Problem works.

Sarah and Jonah got the concept quickly, but like recent occupants of a trance, they didn't see how it might apply to them. I offered them the possibility that they were having trouble accepting the higher level of success and abundance, and that their arguments were not about sexual flirtation or any of the other things they were squabbling about. Perhaps those subjects needed to be addressed, I said, but not until they got the bigger picture into focus. The bigger picture was the tendency to sabotage their good feelings because they were not accustomed to receiving the higher level of abundance and success. I suggested that through squandering their energy on criticism and the sexual flirtation issue, they were keeping themselves trapped in their Zone of Excellence. Sarah and Jonah greeted my interpretation skeptically but were curious enough to stick with me a little longer.

As we explored together, Sarah gave more details on how she was experiencing the situation. Right after the quarterly earnings report, she had suddenly found herself being extremely critical of herself as well as of Jonah. "Out of nowhere," she said, "I would suddenly start making mental lists of all my shortcomings and Jonah's, too. Then I couldn't keep from starting to criticize Jonah out loud. Then, he would start in on me and we'd be off and running."

What about those accusations of sexual flirtation, though? Where were they coming from? I knew from past experience that when you hide feelings inside yourself, you start seeing them in other people. This is especially true with sexual feelings. I wondered if Sarah had felt a sexual attraction to someone else, hidden those feelings away deep inside her, and suddenly started focusing on her husband's sexual feelings. If so, she wouldn't be the first (or the five millionth) person to do this. It's called *projection,* and there are dozens of chapters in the psychology textbooks on how it works. Simply put, if you have some emotion within you that you don't know how to manage, you seal that emotion away and start trying to manage other people's versions of it. I decided to play the hunch.

Think back to before all this started. Did you have some sexual feelings of your own that you hid down inside you?

There was an electric feeling in the room. They both seemed stunned, with a deer-in-the-headlights look of wide-eyed astonishment on their faces. Then, Sarah broke the silence with an attack on the messenger. She shot me a hostile glance and sneered, "So you think this is all my fault?"

"Absolutely not," I said. "This is not about fault or blame or anything like that. It's about helping you find out how things work in your relationship." Jonah suddenly chimed in with an observation: "I'm remembering that party." She rolled her eyes, as in "Here we go again." I asked them to tell me about it, and suddenly the whole scene was illuminated.

They had attended a large party at the home of some friends. It so happened that Sarah's very favorite wine was being freely poured, and in the course of the evening she'd had, in her words, "more than my share." She had become engrossed in a conversation with a young man who had just finished his MBA at the local university. On the way home from the party she and Jonah got into a huge argument. It started when she made mention of the young man's ease with communicating his feelings. Jonah's difficulty with communicating about his emotions was a frequent subject in their arguments.

"Let's return to that moment, and see if we can figure out what was really going on," I said. I suggested that there was something completely innocent but very important about her interaction with the young man. I asked Sarah to tune in to her deepest feelings and look for anything she might be hiding from herself. It took only a few seconds for it to emerge. Tears came, and she said that her conversation with the young man had triggered a deep sadness in her. She despaired that she would never have the kind of easy flow of communication with Jonah that she felt with the young man. It also triggered gloomy midlife thoughts that she was forty-five and "over the hill," and might not ever experience the kind of deep emotional intimacy she yearned for in her marriage.

When people communicate at the deepest level, as Sarah was doing, it inspires others to drop into that level themselves. Jonah listened with rapt attention, and when he spoke it was to say, in a hushed tone, "I never realized how much that meant to you. Whenever that subject came up, I just heard it as criticism."

I summarized: "You felt attracted to the young man because you were connecting with him on the emotional level. You really want that kind of connection with Jonah, but you despair of ever getting it. If you don't get that, you're going to fail to accomplish one of your biggest life goals. That's big stuff. No wonder you started accusing Jonah of being attracted to a couple of the young women on your staff." She nodded in agreement. Jonah leaned forward and said, "To be fair, I'd have to say I *am* attracted to them, although I would never act on it. They both have a kind of easygoing quality to them. Sarah and I used to have that when we were younger. I miss that. Everything is always such a big deal now, because we always have to be thinking about money and the business and the consequences of every little thing." When he said this I noticed a new quality of attention on Sarah's face. This was exactly the kind of communication she was looking for from him. When he spoke to her from that deeper place in himself, he became the man she wanted to be married to, inviting her into the place where her dreams could be fulfilled.

Here's something I've learned from many experiences of helping people resolve conflicts. Under the surface of most conflicts, you'll find that the warring parties are actually feeling the same deeper emotions. Two people may be locked in an angry conflict for weeks. When they get beneath the roiled surface of the issue, however, they discover that the real issue is that they're both sad about something they've both kept hidden. They've been so locked into proving each other wrong that they haven't taken a moment to contact the true heart of the issue. Sarah and Jonah were a living example of this problem. Once I see people communicating about the deeper feelings, I know that it's possible for the miracle of rebirth to occur in the relationship. Now they're communicating as allies, not as enemies, and when people do that, real-life miracles are possible.

Over the next couple of sessions, we worked on getting all those deeper feelings up into the light. There was sadness, and there were a number of fears they shared. They were afraid their lives were slipping away from them, swallowed up by all the long hours spent on the business, on entertaining clients, on designing and building their dream house, and on the other time demands of their big lives.

THE FIRST STEP TO WHOLENESS:
DISCOVERING YOUR STORY

Earlier in this chapter I mentioned that integrity is really about wholeness and completeness. An integrity breach occurs when we do something that separates us from the wholeness of ourselves or other people. To find these breaches and restore wholeness, we need to get good at asking questions like these:

Where do I feel out of integrity with myself?

What is keeping me from feeling complete and whole?

What important feelings am I not letting into my awareness?

Where in my life am I not telling the full truth?

Where in my life have I not kept my promises?

In my relationship with _____, what do I need to say or do to feel complete and whole?

Questions such as these will lift you out of the limiting story that you've been living in. Almost all of us have a story about why we don't access our genius. When we are within that story, it is very difficult to know that it's just a story. What makes those stories seem so real (hard to recognize as "just stories") is that they were being told before we were born. We're born into stories that keep us from accessing our genius. We grow up among those stories and become like fish that aren't aware of the water they're swimming in.

For example, in one family the story might be that genius leads to irresponsibility. There was old Uncle George, who left his wife and seven kids behind to go off seeking his genius in the wilds of Fiji. He was never heard from again, except in one tantalizing photo he sent of himself grinning like a loon in the company of a native dance troupe. In another family the story might be that genius leads to madness. There's old Aunt Cecily who retreated to her room in 1927 to write poetry and for the next forty years could always be heard cackling and howling up there. In another family the story might be that genius leads to poverty and decrepitude. Cousin Freddie spent his life trying to perfect an engine that ran on club soda and was forced to support himself in his old age by becoming a paperboy. Those stories are passed down from one generation to the next, to protect members of the clan from straying too far outside the confines of their zones of incompetence, competence, and excellence.

Whatever your story is, the first task is to find it. Identify your family story of why you shouldn't access your genius. Once you've identified it, the next task is to lose your fascination with it. Don't give yourself a hard time for being fascinated with it; you were born into it just like the rest of us. Just become more fascinated with the story of your Big Leap into the Zone of Genius. Gradually this new fascination with genius will replace the unconscious fascination with the old programmed story.

THE ATTITUDE

I hope you're not feeling overwhelmed by the complexity of the task. If so, remember that it comes down to specific things you do, none of which takes long in clock time. For example, it takes only ten seconds to locate and acknowledge a feeling in your body such as sadness or fear. It takes only a few seconds to communicate a specific truth to another person, a truth that can restore wholeness to a relationship that's felt incomplete for years. As you go about your discoveries, you'll benefit from adopting an attitude of wonder instead of blame. In other words, being lighthearted about noticing your Upper Limit behaviors will help you make progress faster than if you criticize yourself for every little thing. When I maintain an attitude of cheerful wonder and keen interest toward my faults and flaws, I see them dissolve and transform much more rapidly than when I give myself a hard time about them.

If you're willing to adopt a playful attitude toward yourself and your shortcomings, you can make extraordinarily rapid progress. It's easier to chuckle over things than to fret over them, and chuckling is much more fun for the people around you. Here's an example of lighthearted wonder: In one of my advanced groups for executives, some of the participants began referring to the Upper Limit Problem by its acronym, ULP. They pronounced it as in "Gulp." One of the group's members said he remembered comic-book characters saying "ULP!" when they encountered something unexpected. It didn't take long for "ULP" to catch on. Soon, people were saying things like "I had an ULP today" and "I caught myself in the midst of an ULP this afternoon."

I encourage you to adopt this kind of playfulness toward all your ULPs. An attitude of playful wonder is characteristic of people when they're operating in the Zone of Genius. For inspiration, I keep an autographed picture of Albert Einstein on the wall of my office. My wife gave it to me for my birthday some years ago; it's one of my most treasured possessions. The look of wonder in his eyes reminds me to keep seeking the deepest truths about life, and to do my seeking in the spirit of play, not work.

ACTION STEPS

Here's what I recommend for daily action steps. These specific actions will keep you on track and on the fast track to living in your Zone of Genius.

Make a commitment to keeping an attitude of wonder and play while learning about your Upper Limit behaviors. Say this sentence in your mind as often as you like. It expresses the attitude I'd like you to embody: *I commit to discovering my Upper Limit behaviors, and to having a good time while I'm learning about them.* You can learn a lot more with a spirit of wonder and enjoyment than you can with an attitude of criticism.

Make a list of your Upper Limit behaviors. Here are some of the most common ones:

- Worrying

- Blame and criticism

- Getting sick or hurt

- Squabbling

- Hiding significant feelings

- Not keeping agreements

- Not speaking significant truths to the relevant people.

(If you're mad at John, he's the relevant person to talk to. It doesn't help to tell Fred that you're mad at John.)

- Deflecting. (Brushing off compliments is a good example of deflecting)

When you notice yourself doing one of the things on your Upper Limit list, such as worrying, or failing to communicate some truth, shift your attention to the real issue: expanding your capacity for abundance, love, and success.

Consciously let yourself make more room in your awareness for abundance, love, and success. Use the resources of your whole being, not just your mind. For example, feel more love in your chest and heart area. Savor the body feeling, as well as the mental satisfaction, of success and abundance.

Embrace a new story that tells about your adventures in your Zone of Genius. Find a new mythology, or make up one of your own, that shows you enjoying your life in the full radiance of your expressed potential.

In the next chapter we'll explore how to live your new story. You'll see how to get beyond all the fears and spells that cause us to limit our potential. You'll learn how to build a new foundation for yourself, a strong base from which you can thrive in your Zone of Genius.

FOUR

Building a New Home in Your Zone of Genius

How to Make Every Moment an Expression of Your Genius

In this chapter you'll discover the answers to two main questions:

What is my genius?

How can I bring forth my genius in ways that serve others and myself at the same time?

Those who have the courage to discover and bring forth their genius break through to unparalleled heights of productivity and life satisfaction.

Discovering your Zone of Genius is your life's Big Leap. Everything up until now has been about hops, not leaps. Hopping, though it seems safe, is actually hazardous to your health. If you confine yourself to hops, you run the risk of rusting from the inside out. I know. I caught myself, halfway through my life, in the very act of rusting. There I was, hopping along in my Zone of Excellence, when suddenly I became aware of a dull and sluggish feeling deep within me. I couldn't figure out what it was at first. As I tuned in to it, I realized it had been there for months, maybe years.

I had gotten to a place in my life where I could almost sleepwalk through doing all the things that kept me successful—writing books, giving speeches, coaching executives, teaching seminars. I did them and did them and did them, and the money kept pouring in. Soon there were employees, a big building, three houses, and an army of support personnel that needed to be fed. I remember well the day it all imploded on me.

I got off the plane, exhausted from a grueling trip during which I'd given many talks and seminars—nineteen cities in twenty-one days. I stopped by the office on the way home, and there I encountered glum looks on the faces of my accountant and administrative director. They announced that taxes were due, and that because of a cash-flow shortfall I needed to borrow $120,000 from myself to pay our taxes. I felt like a hunter-gatherer returning with a wild boar for the campfire, expecting high-fives and a hot dinner, only to be told I also owed a couple of buffalo. I slunk home, dejected and irritated, and there I found that my garage-door opener had died. Leaving my car in the driveway, I trudged out to get the mail. The first thing I pulled out was a big envelope emblazoned with this headline: "Congratulations on Turning 50! Here Is Your Free AARP Card!" I paused to digest the significance of this moment, and that's when I became aware of the sluggish, dull feeling deep within me.

At first I worried it might be a medical problem, so I started by getting a thorough workup. I discovered that I was in the best of health, except for twenty extra pounds of prosperity-induced padding, the effects of too many well-paid after-dinner speeches. Finding I was in good health meant I had to take a deeper look. When I did, I found the source of my rust, and that discovery changed my life. The source was hidden in plain sight: it was the Upper Limit Problem I knew so well. In spite of knowing a lot about it intellectually, I had gotten comfortably numb in my Zone of Excellence. So comfortably numb, in fact, that the ULP had sneaked up and gotten me. Without realizing it, I'd worn such a comfortable rut in my Zone of Excellence that I had overlooked the beckoning calls of my Zone of Genius. Fortunately, I got the message in time. I want to make sure you do, too.

We all need to be on the lookout for signs of our Upper Limit Problem every day of our lives. It's a constant quest, because we're always raising the bar on ourselves. The better we get, the better we want to be. Part of us wants very much to live in our Zone of Genius. Yet at the same time, we're tied down by forces around us. The people around us want us to stay in our Zone of Excellence. We're a lot more reliable there.

I just returned from a meeting that included a man and a woman who were both Harvard MBAs. Getting an MBA is a great achievement: it takes dedication, brilliance, and hard work. However, it's a hop, not a leap. You and I probably know plenty of brilliant, dedicated, hardworking people who hopped through difficult hoops such as getting a Harvard MBA. You and I also know that most of them never made the Big Leap into their Zone of Genius. If you want to take a close look at this phenomenon, all you need to do is attend a class reunion.

Not long ago I gathered with a number of the people who got their Ph.D.'s at Stanford while I was there doing the same in the 1970s. The Counseling Psychology program was designed to train leaders in the field, so most of us took up careers as university professors or private-practice psychologists. We were gathered to celebrate one of our professors, now retiring after a long and fruitful career. It was a festive occasion fueled by goodwill, fond memories, and a free-flowing bar. After a few glasses of cheer, though, deeper feelings came pouring forth. The evening soured temporarily into a complaint fest.

Out of a roomful of fifty or so people, only a half dozen of us seemed to be genuinely happy with the way our lives were going. The professors in the group complained of sluggish bureaucracies and administrations that didn't support their research. They complained of pitiful salaries and the dire shortage of faculty parking spaces. The theme was "If it weren't for _____ , I could be doing what I really want to do." The private-practice therapists had their own set of complaints: slow payments by insurance companies and the ever-expanding quagmire of paperwork. The therapists made a lot more money than the professors, so the therapists' complaints were flavored more by financial woes. They spoke bitterly of greedy ex-spouses, high alimony payments, long hours, ungrateful clients, exhaustion, and burnout. The theme was "If it weren't for _____ , I could be doing what I really want to do."

What was especially striking to me was that the professors envied the private-practice people, who in turn were envious of the professors. From the professors' viewpoint, the private-practice people had it made, with their big salaries, plush offices, and absence of faculty meetings. To the private-practice crowd, though, the professors were the ones with the cushy jobs. They got a steady paycheck, free office space, short hours, and plenty of time to write.

As the evening wore on, I listened to one tale of thwarted hopes after another. Finally I was jolted by an insight: none of these complaints were actually caused by pigheaded bureaucrats, lack of parking spaces, ungrateful clients, or anything of the sort. In other words, none of these brilliant, well-meaning people were upset for the reasons they thought they were.

Their complaints were all symptoms of not taking the Big Leap! From this perspective, every story took on a different meaning, and I began asking a different question in response to each person's story.

After listening to a complaint, I would ask, "If outside influences like money or insurance companies or bureaucrats were not a problem, what would you really love to be doing?" I learned a lot from what each person told me. First, almost everyone could tell me clearly what they'd love to be doing. Their answers included things like:

- I'd love to have time to write the book I've been wanting to write.

- I'd love to create videos so more people could get access to the techniques I use.

- I'd love to have more of an impact in the world.

What caught my attention, though, was the emotional tone behind those statements. Every time, the person's face took on an expression of longing tinged with hope or burdened by despair. Longing is a persistent, lingering feeling of wanting something you can't quite get or something you've judged unobtainable. If you think there's still a possibility of attaining it, your longing is flavored by hope. If you think it's unobtainable, your longing sinks into a bog of despair. Longing was what I was hearing in every one of those conversations.

Here's the other thing I learned that night. Most people have a carefully crafted, well-justified story about why they can't take their Big Leap. For one person it was about the family: "I can't possibly take the time to write ["make a video," etc.] because my family needs me." For another person it was about stress: "I tried getting up at 5 a.m. for a while to work on my book, but I couldn't do that and do a good job with my 6 p.m. and 7 p.m. therapy clients." For others it was purely about the money: "I can't do what I really want to do because I might not make as much money doing it."

As I listened to these stories, I would sometimes hear the real fears emerge. There is a huge fear underneath every complaint: *If I took the Big Leap into my Zone of Genius, I might fail. What if I really opened up to my true genius and found that my genius wasn't good enough?* Better to keep the genie in the bottle and coast along in the Zone of Excellence. That way I don't have to risk taking a Big Leap and finding it isn't good enough. That way I don't have to risk discovering the ugly possibility that I don't *have* a Zone of Genius.

Unless you're very lucky or very enlightened, you're likely to hear those nattering voices and feel those nagging fears within you. They're part of the deal. I won't try to talk you out of them, and you shouldn't try to talk yourself out of them, either. Just notice the voices and feel the fears. That's all you need to do with them. You don't need to rid yourself of them. Where would they go, anyway? All you need to do is acknowledge them, wave to them, let them know you're aware of them. Then get busy learning to live in your Zone of Genius.

YOUR GENIUS COMMITMENT

Take a new step with me, one that will begin to anchor you in your Zone of Genius. Recall the questions I asked you at the beginning of chapter 1. Now I want to ask you a new question that will turn on the turbojets for your Big Leap.

I want you to make that Big Leap into your Zone of Genius. I've found an exhilaration there—a constant sense of purposeful joy—that nothing else can compare to. In your Zone of Genius, you don't feel like you're working. Even though the time you spend there produces great financial abundance, you do not feel that you are expending effort to produce it. In your Zone of Genius, work doesn't feel like work.

In your Zone of Genius, time feels completely different. Time seems to expand to support your activities. You have plenty of time to do what you most want to do. You'll learn more about this unusual phenomenon in chapter 6, "Living in Einstein Time." For right now, though, just know that in your Zone of Genius, time doesn't fly—it flows.

How about it? Will you make a commitment to living in your Zone of Genius all the time? If you do that, I can promise you as much real-life magic as you care to experience.

In coaching people to discover their genius, I've found that it's essential to begin with a commitment to living in your Zone of Genius. Your commitment must come before you know how to make good on it. The image that comes to mind is from the third Indiana Jones movie, in which Indy must step out into thin air, in a gesture of commitment, before a bridge magically appears beneath his feet. The power of your commitment brings forth the means necessary for you to live in your Zone of Genius. If you will make a powerful, sincere commitment—a vow that you really want to live your life in the Zone of Genius—your journey will be blessed with uncommon good fortune at all the twists and turns of the road. Commitment has that power.

I invite you to make your commitment right at this moment. Make a private deal between you and the universe, a formal commitment to living in your Zone of Genius.

Here's the sentence I use when working with people:

I commit to living in my Zone of Genius, now and forever.

Repeat it softly to yourself a few times, noticing how it feels to you. Then say it out loud a few times. Savor the different words and sounds of the sentence. When you are ready to make your formal commitment, speak the sentence from your heart, as a formal contract between you and the universe.

THE GENIUS QUESTIONS

Your sincere commitment is the entry gate to the Zone of Genius. Now that you've stepped out into the unknown, the bridge can appear under your feet. The bridge to your Zone of Genius is a set of questions to ask yourself. Actually, *ask* doesn't quite capture the flavor of how I want you to use the questions. I want you to wonder about them. These questions are designed to bring forth hidden treasures from deep inside you. Wonder is the tool that invites these treasures up into the light. To wonder about something is to explore with an open mind and an open heart. *Wonder* is defined as "amazed admiration," so be sure to do your wondering with the attitude that your discoveries will be amazing and admirable.

Genius Question no. 1

Here's the first Genius Question:

What do I most love to do?
(I love it so much I can do it for long stretches of time without getting tired or bored.)

When I was first figuring out how my own genius worked and how to get established in my Zone of Genius, I spent a lot of time wondering how to distinguish my genius from my excellence. I finally realized a big key to it: my genius is connected to what I most love to do. That's why I want you to wonder about what you most love to do.

After wondering about it myself for more than a week, I began to get clear on what I most love to do. It's translating big, important, life-changing concepts into simple, practical things people can use. It's also dreaming up, or download-ing directly from the source, those same kinds of useful, life-changing tools. I've never quite been able to figure out whether I'm incubating and launching those concepts myself, or opening my gates to let in information from a different dimension. Perhaps it doesn't really matter, as long as it turns out to be useful.

Kathlyn and I coached two women who were struggling in their corporate consulting business. They had both been successful on their own, and had brought their businesses to-gether to increase revenues and reduce expenses. The synergy didn't produce the desired effect, though, in terms of creat-ing additional revenue, so they sought our counsel on what was holding them back. Rather than trying to figure out what could be done on the level of expenses, revenues, and other business-related items, we focused on love. We asked them, "What do you most love to do in your business?" Their answer revealed the problem and the solution. Rhonda and Cynthia both lit up at the question, and told us that the main reason they had wanted to work together rather than separately was that they loved the spirit of play that each of them brought to their work. In their individual consulting practices, they had each become well known for bringing a sense of play to seemingly dull corporate seminars on budgeting and goal-setting. They figured that if they integrated their businesses, a quantum enhancement of that spirit of play would bring even more success. After hearing this, we took a few minutes to examine their Web site and their slick, colorful brochure. The missing element was clear at a glance. "Where is the spirit of play in your materials?" we asked. The Web site and brochure were both beautifully produced and professional-looking, but they were devoid of any kind of playful aspect. Even their mission statement was worded in dull corporate-speak. Rhonda and Cynthia suddenly realized that in trying to become more "corporate" and professional, they had left out the key ingredient. They saw that leaving the play out of their work had created an integrity glitch that was reflected in the lack of business. We suggested that they revise their Web site and brochure while they themselves were feeling a spirit of play. If they stopped feeling that spirit, we counseled, they should stop and come back to it later when they were feeling playful again. We heard later that their business had taken a healthy upturn after they put the play back where it belongs in their world.

So, enter the outskirts of your Zone of Genius by asking yourself what you most love to do. Wonder about this until you have a clearly forming sense of it in your body. You don't have to know it clearly or specifically yet. You just need to feel the glimmer of it in your inner world.

Genius Question no. 2

Now let's render "what I most love" into something much more specific. Here's the second Genius Question I'd like you to ponder:

What work do I do that doesn't seem like work?
(I can do it all day long without ever feeling tired or bored.)

There's something at the very heart of the work you identify when you ask yourself this question. When you're doing this certain thing (and not burdened with the pressures and irritations of running a business), you are at your very happiest. When you're doing it, you think "*This* is why I do the work I do."

I counseled an executive in his mid-fifties, Bob, who had risen through the ranks in a major corporation, a few months after his promotion to CEO. He came to me because, as he put it, "I haven't had a decent night's sleep since I took over the job. Something's wrong and I can't figure out what it is." I flew out to Chicago to see if we could find out what was bugging him. Genius Question no. 2 turned the key. When I asked him what aspect of his work didn't feel like work to him, he told me that what he loved best was wandering around, talking to other executives, for ten seconds or five minutes, about whatever was on their mind. He said he got more done in those casual conversations than in formal meetings. Suddenly the light dawned. He said, "You know, I haven't done that a single time since I got promoted to CEO." The reason was partly logistical; he was now in a suite of offices that was separate from where he did his "wandering around." He had also been so inundated with new data that he had spent most of his time trying to get it all into his head. He made a commitment to start wandering around again, and even did an hour of it while I was there. I flew back home that night, and heard the next day that he got a good night's sleep.

If you're like most of us, you feel sad or irritated about the amount of your precious time that gets eaten up in the necessary trivia of your day. As you get more successful, it's common to feel a mounting pressure about this issue, an unnatural hurry-up that feels unhealthy to your well-being. I believe that the sense of mounting pressure is the call to live in your Zone of Genius. I've seen it disappear with miraculous speed when people opened up to wondering about what their true genius might be. If you're feeling any of that kind of pressure, you've made it to the right book, and I'm very glad you did.

Genius Question no. 3

Here is the third question I'd like you to entertain in that vast playground where your heart meets your mind:

In my work, what produces the highest ratio of abundance and satisfaction to amount of time spent?

(Even if I do only ten seconds or a few minutes of it, an idea or a deeper connection may spring forth that leads to huge value.)

By asking myself this question, I discovered that part of my genius is the free play of ideas in my mind. It's the ability to let ideas tumble and transform, free of criticism and censure, until something useful emerges. I've had projects where I've incubated and tumbled an idea for years before the fruitful outcome came forth, but I've also had experiences in which a few seconds devoted to free mind play have turned into millions in revenue. I never know exactly where it's going to lead to or whether it's going to lead anywhere at all. That's part of the excitement of it—not knowing—and it may be that not knowing is the key to the success of the process.

Over and over I hear executives, in fits of frustration, give voice to complaints like this: "If I could just sit in my office and think for an hour without being interrupted, I could produce amazing results." I don't make that complaint anymore (although I used to hear it come off my lips fairly often). For many years now, I've spent at least an hour every day meditating and letting my mind roam freely. Setting aside time to do this every day is a practical way to make good on my commitment to one of my highest-priority activities.

The answer you come up with may be entirely different, but I promise you, there is some essential aspect of the work you do that produces the greatest payoff. Perhaps it's connecting with your staff or your customers in a certain kind of way. Or perhaps it's simply picking up the phone and having a certain kind of conversation with a key person. Whatever it is, I want you to find it, and I want you to put the highest priority on doing some of it every day. In my own case, I've found it helpful to structure it into my day. This morning, and every other morning for the last couple of decades, I sat down for a half hour of meditation and free mind play. I do this before I engage in any "official" work such as e-mail, writing, or project planning. To me, if something has the highest priority, it means I do it first.

It takes a certain ruthlessness to set a priority and stick to it. For example, some years ago I worked with Nancy, a woman who had a burning desire to write mystery novels. She also had three kids, a husband, and a big commitment to activities in her church and community. Nancy had published one novel that did well enough to make the publisher want more, but not well enough for her to hire household help or a personal assistant. In our first and only session, I asked Nancy to describe how she spent her day. She told me that after getting her kids and husband off to work, she straightened up the house and took care of infrastructure stuff like paying bills and making grocery lists. Then, she said, "if I've got any energy left, I sit down and write for an hour or two. If not, I take a nap and try to write for an hour or so before the kids start coming home."

I summarized Nancy's priorities, based on how she spent her day. "Your family is your highest priority, right?" She

agreed. "Your second priority is housework and infrastructure, and your third priority is writing."

"No!" she exclaimed. "Writing is much higher priority than
housework and that sort of thing." I pointed out that if that
were true, she would do her writing *before* she did the house-
related things. Her reply was the key to resolving the whole
issue. She said, "But I can't sit down to write unless I've got a
clean house and things taken care of."

"Sure, you can," I said. "You just think you have to get that
other stuff done first. Where did you get an idea like that?"
She said, "But what if my husband came back from work and
found a dirty house and me sitting up there writing?"

"He'd find a wife who put a higher priority on her creative
expression than she did on keeping the house clean. Do you
think he'd be upset about that?" "Not really," she said. "I
think he'd actually like it." As our conversation developed, it
became clear that she was holding herself hostage to housework for Upper Limit reasons. Nancy's unconscious mind
had constructed a doom scenario of what would occur if she
went all the way into her Zone of Genius. In her imagination,
if she put her full attention into her writing, she'd neglect her
family, and they would languish in the absence of her attention. Nancy began to see the absurdity of that way of thinking. She also discovered the real fear that was underneath it
all: that if she made a big commitment to her creativity, she
might fail on a bigger scale. If she stayed small, she could
avoid the possibility of big rejection.

We covered another important chunk of territory in the session. Nancy also realized that she had a major fear of outshining her siblings. One of four girls, she had received mixed reactions from her sisters when her first novel came out. One sister had been thrilled and very supportive, while the other two showed various signs of jealousy and competitiveness. Her unconscious mind's solution had been to put the brakes on her creativity and let herself get consumed by housework and other pressures of daily life, in hopes that the strains in the relationship with her sisters would disappear.

I suggested another possibility to Nancy: Don't hold yourself back to keep your sisters from feeling jealous. Go all the way, and inspire them with your full expression. You can't manage their feelings. Their feelings are their business. They'd probably be just as jealous if you bought a new refrigerator, so you might as well go all the way and write a few best sellers. That way, they'll be jealous about something worth being jealous about. They might just go in a positive direction, though, and get inspired to do something magnificent in their own lives.

As we wound up our session, I gave her a homework assignment: for one week, sit down and write *before* doing any of the house-related tasks. I told her, "After you get your husband and kids out the door, force yourself to go up and write for an hour or two. Break the pattern. Your mind may try to get you back in the old pattern. It might scream 'No, no, no! Wash those dishes, put those clothes in the dryer before you write. If you don't, civilization will collapse!' Just politely thank your mind for the unsolicited advice, and then sit down and write anyway."

I never saw Nancy again in person, although she called me a couple of times to report on her progress. The task she'd taken on was not an easy one. She had spent many years being programmed to do things a certain way. In her growing-up years, her mother had been a stay-at-home mom whose house was always spotless. It took her many weeks to get her literary life up to a higher priority than her domestic chores. There were more than a few days when she fell back into the old pattern, but over the next year she was able to move her creative activities up to where they belonged on her priority list.

Genius Question no. 4

Take a deep breath, and expand to embrace a new conception of yourself. The fourth Genius Question invites you to think of who you are in most unusual terms. It asks you to identify a unique and priceless gift you carry within yourself. Your exploration into this aspect of yourself is not about self-flattery or expansion of your ego. It's a clear-eyed look at a deep, innermost quality, with the intention of applying that quality to make your own life and the lives of others more valuable. Here's the question:

What is my unique ability?
(There's a special skill I'm gifted with. This unique ability, fully
realized and put to work, can provide enormous benefits to me
and any organization I serve.)

We're in search of the deepest essentials here; if you look
into the essence of who you really are at the deepest level,
you'll find a unique gift you've been blessed with. That gift is
your greatest contribution to the people around you. It's the
pinnacle skill of your working life. You can also use it to great
benefit in your nonworking life. (The ability is not unique in
the whole world. There may be millions of people who have
it. However, it's usually unique in your particular circle or
work setting.)

Do you know what your unique ability is? You may have
discovered it already, but if you haven't, I'd like to show you
how to find it. First, let me share with you an image I like to
use. Have you seen a set of those little Russian dolls? When
you open the big doll there's a smaller one inside it, and
hidden within that doll there's an even smaller one. Using
that image, think of your unique ability as a skill within a
skill within a skill. Here's what I mean: your unique ability
is usually camouflaged inside a larger skill you possess. You
may not even realize that your unique ability is what is driving your success in applying the larger skill.

For example, I didn't learn about my unique ability until
well into my thirties. I had been using it all along, but it was

like water to a fish: I had taken it so much for granted that I didn't know it was a definable skill that could be described and refined. I knew I had a skill in helping people solve problems. I didn't get any formal training in therapy skills until I was twenty-four, but according to a family story, I had an early leaning in that direction. I set up a cardboard-box "office" in my grandmother's living room when I was a preschooler. I told my family that my job was to help people solve problems. According to the story, I was very clear that I didn't handle medical problems. They could take those to an ordinary doctor. I told them I specialized in problems around the house. Since I grew up in a small southern town with no psychiatrists, psychologists, and such, I haven't a clue where I might have picked this idea up. (I should also mention that this first foray of mine into the consulting business was an utter flop: none of my family members ever took advantage of my services. In retrospect, I can forgive them for being reluctant to consult with a therapist who wore short pants and commuted to work on a tricycle.)

My unique ability occurs within the larger skill of helping people solve problems. The best way I can describe it is that I can be with people in a certain way that enables them to come up with creative solutions they hadn't thought of before. I can create a space that brings forth innovative solutions from inside myself or from people I'm working with. I can feel this ability inside me right now. It's a feeling of respect for the creative process, coupled with a nonjudgmental listening for something new to emerge. I can wait patiently as long as it takes for a new solution to emerge. Possibly because I'm willing to wait for as long as it takes, it usually doesn't take long.

Let me give you a real-life example of how this ability works. I consulted once with the top two executives of a Fortune 500 company. They had gotten into a conflict about whether to build a new factory in South America. By the time I got called in, they had been at loggerheads for two weeks. The conflict had erupted into emotional displays that were unsettling to the other executives. The first thing I asked them was whether they would be willing to have a creative solution emerge from our conversation, whether it took two minutes or two days. They said they would be, so the second question I asked them was "What do you think is really going on here?" This question confused them, and I explained that whenever a conflict had gone on as long as theirs had, there was almost always some other factor that was the real cause of the problem. They said they understood, but they had no idea what it might be.

Here's where I put my ability into play. I said, "Then let's just wait and listen. Maybe something will emerge." We sat in silence for ten seconds, then twenty. One of them coughed; then silence reigned again for another twenty seconds or so. Finally the top guy said, "I feel like I'm losing control of the company. If we build this factory down there, it's good-bye to the company we started with. I'm an engineer; I like to walk through the R & D section and shoot the breeze with the engineers anytime I want to." The number-two guy just sat there, looking stunned. "Yeah," number one continued, "I used to be able to stand in the parking lot and see the whole business. I liked that feeling. It felt manageable. Now we're growing so fast I see employees in the halls I haven't even met. It scares me."

Finally, number two said, "I get it. I couldn't figure out what was going on with you. Why didn't you tell me that before?"

Number one raised his palms in a gesture of helplessness: "I didn't know it myself until a moment ago." A few minutes later they came up with an innovative solution: build the factory in South America as planned, but expand the research and development functions they would need there and base them at their present headquarters. That way, the head guy could continue his walk-arounds among the engineers and have the parts of the business he loved close to home.

In business, especially these days, you simply can't afford to have those kinds of conflicts go on for long. Conflicts cost money; they delay key decisions and turn speed-to-market into a molasses-drip morass. One reason for the conflict between my two executives was that they hadn't opened up the kind of space between them that allowed a deeper communication to emerge. Once it came out, the problem was resolved quickly. Building the new factory became a business decision, not an emotional issue.

A serendipitous event occurred while I was working on this section of the book. I caught the sounds of my two granddaughters, Imogen and Elsie (age ten and twelve, respectively) playing in the pool with one of their friends, all under the watchful eye of my wife, Kathlyn. To me, the sound of kids playing is one of the sweetest in life; the squeals coming from the backyard were so delightful that I left the quiet of my den and went to work out back so I could be closer to the action.

It wasn't long before the girls swam over to the pool's edge and asked me what I was working on. I told them I was writing a book about the Upper Limit Problem. Elsie and Imogen nodded (the ULP having been part of their vocabulary much of their lives). Elsie's friend, Hannah, asked, "What's that?" It gave me an opportunity to hear how a twelve-year-old would explain it to another twelve -year-old. Without missing a beat, Elsie said, "If you don't know it's OK to feel good and have a good time, you'll do something to mess up when things are going well." I was typing furiously, trying to capture every word. Hannah asked for an example, and Elsie thought for a moment, giving my fingers a chance to catch up. Finally she said, "You remember when we were playing dodgeball during recess last week, and that kid Frankie broke in and kicked the ball over the fence?" Hannah nodded: "He does that sort of stuff all the time." "Well," Elsie said, "he's got an Upper Limit Problem. He doesn't know how to just have a good time all the time." Grandfatherly pride aside, I think that's a pretty good definition of the Upper Limit Problem.

Sensing we were on a roll, I told them I was working on a section about unique abilities. I asked them, "What do you think your unique ability is?" I explained that a unique ability was a special gift, something you were really good at that was also helpful to people around you. I was searching for another way to explain it when Elsie chimed in and said, "It's like a superpower, right?" She referenced a movie in which the four heroes each had a superpower they used to help in defeating the forces of evil. Imogen got it right away: "Yeah, like a superpower, only it's real!" I couldn't have thought of a better way to describe it myself.

I asked the girls, "What's your real superpower?" Right away Elsie said, "I can sense other people's feelings."

I readily agreed. Pretty much from her first breath, I've always found her to be one of the most sensitive, aware people I've ever known. Perhaps influenced by what Elsie said, the other two girls claimed similar superpowers. Imogen said her unique ability was knowing when people were angry but trying to hide it. Hannah said her skill was being able to tell if people liked each other. Recalling the dramas of life in junior high school, I told them I thought all those skills would come in very handy.

Now, back to focusing on your own unique ability. I'd like you to be able to speak clearly and articulately about your genius. To do that, I've constructed an activity I use when coaching people on their genius.

ARTICULATING YOUR UNIQUE ABILITY

Here's a way to refine your understanding of your own innate genius. Recalling the image we used earlier about the Russian dolls, let's focus first on the outermost doll. This is the larger skill within which is hidden your innate gift. Anne is the forty-year-old CEO of a Silicon Valley consulting firm. When I asked her about her unique ability, she answered, "Running meetings." That was the outermost of the Russian dolls. Now we went one level further in. I asked, "When you're running meetings, what is it that you're doing when you're at your very best?"

She thought for a moment then said, "One thing is knowing when and how to gracefully cut off a discussion and move along." That gave us a little more detail, but it still was not the essence of the skill. I asked another question: "What gives you the ability to know when to do that?" She paused and reflected, and then said, "I've never thought about this before, but I feel an energy shift in the room and inside me. Something shifts in the room, and I know it's time to move on." Her face began to take on a glow as we discussed this subtler skill. That's one way I can tell when people are homing in on their unique ability. Their faces reflect a sense of wonder and rapt attention. "Now that I think about it," she said, "I've been able to do that since I was a kid. It was a way to stay out of my parents' way when they were getting into one of their fights." She told me that she had grown up in a fairly chaotic family, with a father who drank too much and a mother who resented having to carry the extra weight of responsibility.

The first place most of us use our unique ability is in navigating the tricky shoals of childhood. If you reflect on your unique ability, you'll probably find that it made its appearance early in your life. You used it, probably without being aware of it, to cope with stressful situations and optimize your ability to thrive. My early life was an ideal training ground for a budding therapist and executive coach. My mother struggled with depression after my father's sudden death, and I spent much of my early childhood living with my grandparents. They were wonderful with me, but their relationship with each other was a different story. By the time I arrived on the scene, they had been in a pitched battle for several decades, characterized by constant bickering and periods of uneasy truce. I became a go-between for them in times when communication would stall out completely. Since I was about the only thing they could ever agree on, I was in a unique position to help them paper over the rifts between them and get them talking again.

Anne had refined her unique ability in the heat of similar action. I summarized what I'd heard her say: "You have an ability to feel a certain kind of energy shift in the room and inside you, and tuning in to this energy helps you know what to do."

"That's basically it," she said. I asked her if that ability showed up in other situations. "I don't know," she said, "But it's a good question, because if I can use that wherever I am, I'll always know I'm applying my very best part of me to the job."

That's the payoff I'd like you to get. To do that, I recommend that you deconstruct the set of Russian dolls until you uncover the one that contains your unique ability. Begin with a fundamental statement like this:

I'm at my best when I'm _____

_____.

Let that statement resonate in your mind a few times; then speak it out loud. Discover what you come up with. Perhaps you come up with "I'm at my best when I'm generating ideas on a yellow legal pad" or "I'm at my best when I'm figuring out how to put a team together." Just get a good general statement of what you're doing when you feel you're at your best.

Once you've come up with a simple, clear statement of you at your best, go a little deeper. Use a statement like the following to zoom in for a closer look:

When I'm at my best, the exact thing I'm doing is _____

_____.

Go for a more detailed description, such as "When I'm generating ideas on a yellow legal pad, the exact thing I'm doing is doodling and enjoying the feeling of creating something out of nothing."

Go even deeper with a sentence like this one:

When I'm doing that, the thing I love most about it is ____

_____.

For example, "When I'm doodling and creating something out of nothing, the thing I love most is not knowing where it's going to take me. I love the surprise factor, the excitement of seeing what's going to emerge."

You'll be able to know you're getting closer to your unique ability when you feel an inner glow of wonder and excitement. Even though I've been with hundreds of people as they tapped in to that feeling, I never feel blasé about it. There's something intrinsically enlivening about being with people when they're discovering this depth within themselves. Probably because the process is connected to my own genius, I can engage in it all day long and never get tired. That's what I want for you.

FIVE

Living in Your Zone of Genius

Using the Ultimate Success Mantra to Thrive in Love, Abundance, and Creativity

Once you have broken free of the Upper Limit Problem, your job is to learn to live in the Zone of Genius. It is at first a delicate tightrope walk, which then gets easier as you master the skills required to keep your balance in the new environment. Fortunately, there are shortcuts, learned through the raw life experience of hundreds of people. These shortcuts can save you a great deal of time and trouble. I'll show you how to put them to work in this chapter.

OUT OF THE BOX AND ONTO THE SPIRAL

There's a phrase I use in teaching people how to live in the Zone of Genius: get out of the box and onto the spiral. Here's what I mean by it. I think of the Zone of Genius as a continuous spiral. You go higher and higher every day as you expand your capacity for more love, abundance, and success. It's an upward journey with no upper limit. By contrast, I think of the lower zones as boxes. For example, your Zone of Excellence is a space in which you know how to function so well that you can attain great results without stretching yourself very much. It's a box, though, because ultimately you find yourself stymied and unsatisfied within it. You're doing the same thing over and over, and while it feeds the people around you, it doesn't feed you. You need to get out of any boxes you're in so you can taste the sweet freedom of living on a continuous upward spiral. To do that, a central guiding intention comes in very handy.

THE ULTIMATE SUCCESS MANTRA:
A CENTRAL GUIDING INTENTION

Navigating the upward reaches of a spiral is different from navigating around inside a box. I found that it called for a new set of skills. It took quite a few years of experimentation to refine those skills, but with time I discovered a simple set of shortcuts that will make your learning time much more efficient. The first shortcut is to organize your inner operating system around what I call a Central Guiding Intention. The Central Guiding Intention is a metaprogram I want you to install at the root, or source, of your being. I want you to store it alongside other essential metaprograms such as Relating to Gravity and Eating When Hungry. Your Central Guiding Intention will help you live easefully in your Zone of Genius. The Central Guiding Intention for living in your Zone of Genius is what I call the Ultimate Success Mantra.

Before I show you the Ultimate Success Mantra, let me explain a few key things about how mantras work. A mantra is a sound or idea that you use as a focal point in meditation. In some meditation systems, the mantra is a word or sound from an ancient language such as Sanskrit or Hebrew. In other systems it might be an idea, such as "Focus your awareness on your breathing." I've received instruction in many different forms of meditation, and regardless of whether the practice comes from Buddhist, Christian, Jewish, Muslim, or other sources, the mantra is usually employed the same way. You focus your attention on the mantra. Then, when your attention wanders, you return your attention to the mantra. The mantra gives you a home base to come back to whenever you notice that your mind has taken an excursion into the past or the future. The mantra is designed to help you return to the present moment.

For example, if you're using "Om" as your mantra, you repeat "Om" lightly in your mind. After some repetitions your mind will naturally wander. When you notice that it's wandered, you let go of the thoughts and return to repeating "Om." In Buddhist practices, such as Zen and Vipassana meditation, breath awareness is often used as the mantra. You focus your awareness on the sensations of your breathing; then, when you notice that your attention has wandered off into other thoughts, you gently return your awareness to your breathing.

I've been on meditation retreats in which we've meditated up to fourteen hours a day. In my daily life, I do a much more modest practice of a half hour in the morning and evening. In fourteen hours of meditation, or even a half hour, your mind will wander and then return to the mantra hundreds of times. The art of meditation is in the way you let go of your wander-thoughts and return to the mantra. Specifically, the art is in letting go of the wander-thoughts and returning to the mantra without giving yourself a hard time about wandering. It's common in the beginning stages of meditation to criticize yourself when your mind wanders, to think of meditation as a conflict between your mantra and your wander-thoughts. As your practice matures, though, you usually realize that criticizing yourself for your mind's wandering is just another thought. You let go of it and return to the mantra. Gradually the habit of self-criticism disappears and is replaced by an openhearted feeling of self-acceptance.

That's a key to how I want you to use the Ultimate Success Mantra, or USM. In a moment I'll explain the USM and give you formal instructions for putting it to work in your life. As we get into more details, though, let me emphasize that in all your experiences with the USM, your key to integrating it smoothly and effectively into your life is to be gentle and openhearted with yourself. With that in mind, let's proceed to the specifics.

YOUR ULTIMATE SUCCESS MANTRA

The USM is a comprehensive intention you'll use to center yourself in your Zone of Genius. It's a set of instructions to your conscious and unconscious mind, designed to inform all your actions and decisions. If you use the USM as instructed, your life will gradually conform to the comprehensive intention contained within it. Here it is:

I expand in abundance, success, and love every day, as I inspire those around me to do the same.

Begin to work with the USM right now, in the following way: Say it over a few times in your mind, savoring the comprehensive idea that lives within it. Whisper it to yourself in the quiet of your mind. Let it resonate in the vast reaches of your consciousness.

Now, discover how it resonates in your spoken tones.

Say it out loud a few times, listening to the resonance of the words as well as the idea itself. Later I'll invite you to modify it, if you wish, to your own preferences. For now, though, take it as it is, and try it on as you might slip into a new pair of shoes. Slip into the Universal Success Mantra and take it for an experimental walk in your consciousness. It's the product of more than three decades of refinement with several thousand people, so I know it works wonders with a broad range of successful people. However, that's no guarantee you're going to resonate with it. The only way you'll find that out is through giving it a thorough tryout in your own consciousness.

Here's what the Ultimate Success Mantra does for you on a moment-by-moment basis. It beams a key instruction to your conscious and unconscious mind. It tells you to expand, rather than contract or remain as is, in three key areas of your development: abundance, love, and success. The USM directly counters the Upper Limit Problem, which is based on instructions from long ago to contract or to hold yourself in check. The USM is the antidote to years of conditioning, the ancient programming that convinced your unconscious mind you don't deserve full success. I want you to mount a gentle but unstoppable offensive against that conditioning, and the Universal Success Mantra is the best way I've found to do that.

HOW TO USE THE ULTIMATE SUCCESS MANTRA

I recommend you use the USM in two specific ways: formally, as a meditation practice; and informally, as you go about your daily life. The USM is very powerful, so a little bit of it goes a long way. You don't need to rent a cave in Tibet or devote years to the practice. All you need to do is slip the USM into your thought stream from time to time, and watch the magic unfold in your life.

To use the USM as a formal meditation, find a place where you can sit quietly for five to ten minutes. Close your eyes, and rest for a minute or so until your system settles down. Once every fifteen to twenty seconds, whisper the USM softly to yourself; say the words quietly in your mind, like a faint thought. You don't need to pronounce the words distinctly, as long as you can feel the concept of the USM. It will go like this:

- Whisper the USM softly to yourself. (It takes me five to seven seconds to do this.)

- Pause and rest with an open mind for ten to fifteen seconds. (This is about the time it takes for two slow, easy breaths.)

- Whisper the USM softly to yourself again.

- Pause and rest with an open mind for ten to fifteen seconds.

- Continue like this for five to ten minutes.

- When you feel you're at a good stopping place, pause and rest for a minute or two before returning to your normal activities.

WHAT TO EXPECT

The ten to fifteen seconds of "pause and rest with an open mind" are just as important as saying the USM. You need to give your conscious and unconscious mind a few moments of open space in which to digest this powerful new idea. You also need to give yourself room to bring forth what I call *back-talk* from your old programming. Back-talk is what occurs when your old programming argues with the beautiful new idea you're beaming into the depths of yourself. You say the USM to yourself—*I expand in abundance, success, and love every day, as I inspire those around me to do the same*—and a burst of mind chatter talks back to you with something like "Forget it. You'll never inspire anybody to do anything worthwhile."

Expect plenty of back-talk during those seconds after you've floated the USM through your mind. It's good to make room for the resistance that you (along with the rest of us) have to the powerful idea in the USM to surface. After all, you're overcoming decades of conditioning, and you can't expect that old programming to disappear into the void without a murmur.

Actually, I want you not only to expect back-talk but to encourage it. Back-talk is a good thing, because it lets you know that the USM is working. The back-talk will stop once the USM has permeated your conscious and unconscious mind. Later, when you're firmly established in your Zone of Genius, you'll look back on your resistance like it was a backpack full of rocks you carried without realizing it. Once you take off the extra weight of the backpack, you'll feel so liberated you won't waste much time being concerned with the years you spent carrying it.

Here's how to use the Ultimate Success Mantra informally, as an addition to your daily life. Occasionally throughout the day, float the USM through your mind or speak it out loud. Just slip it into your ordinary thought stream as you move through your day. I also recommend writing it out on three-by-five cards or sticky notes and posting it in various places where you'll see it during the day. I put it in places where I look often, such as the dashboard of my car or a corner of my desk. This will serve to remind you of it during the busy whirl of your day.

A KEY SHORTCUT: THE ENLIGHTENED NO

As you learn to navigate the updrafts of the Genius Spiral, your flight will be smoother if you get nimble at what I call "the Enlightened No." You produce an Enlightened No when you turn down something that doesn't fit into your Zone of

Genius. I call it the Enlightened No because you're saying no in the service of your genius. You're not saying no for all the usual reasons, such as money, dislike, lack of time, and so forth. You're saying no because you've chosen to focus on activities that are clearly in your Zone of Genius. Saying no for that reason even has an inspirational effect on the people you're turning down. I've frequently had people get in touch to thank me for the way I said no to them, because it inspired them to do the same thing in service of their own genius.

I encourage you to look carefully at the number of times you say yes to things that do not fit in your Zone of Genius. Even if they seem beneficial for other reasons, those requests can eat up a great deal of energy that could be better invested in expressing your genius.

Let me give you an example. A while back I had a flurry of requests from a company that had invented several electronic devices it wanted me to endorse. I checked out the devices (they fit broadly into the category of biofeedback machines), and they did indeed appear to be useful. The company offered me fifty thousand dollars and some stock if I would give my endorsement. While on the surface it looked like easy money for endorsing something that could help people, I took some time to think it over. In discussing the matter with Kathlyn, I got a great reminder of why for the last twenty-eight years since I met her I've awakened every day feeling like the luckiest man on earth. She listened to my description of the gadgets and the company and the deal they were offering, and without blinking an eye she asked, "Does it fit in your Zone of Genius?" The question took me so by surprise that I burst out laughing. "No," I said, "except maybe the fifty thousand dollars part!"

Here's where the magic of saying an Enlightened No comes into play. I sent them an e-mail that explained why I was turning them down. In part it said, "I've been really benefiting in recent years from focusing on activities that are in what I call my Zone of Genius. These are things that I'm uniquely suited to do, and which serve my highest purposes for my life. While I like the people I've met from your company, and while I think the devices are useful, I'm going to turn down your generous offer because it doesn't fit in the sweet spot of my Zone of Genius." About an hour after I sent the e-mail, I got a call from the head of the company. He said something like "You would not believe the discussion that came out of getting your e-mail." He said that the executive team had already planned an off-site to focus on this topic for themselves. Would I be willing to hire myself out for the day to work with them on it? I told him I didn't have time to do that, because I was firmly ensconced in my Zone of Genius every day, writing a book (the one you're holding) that explained everything I knew about the subject. If he could be patient for six or eight months, I'd be happy to send him a copy and we could talk about a seminar for his organization.

Most opportunities to say an Enlightened No do not come attached to compelling amounts of cash. It doesn't matter, though, because it's not about the cash value of the thing you're saying no to. It's about strengthening your commitment to living in your Zone of Genius. Each time you say an Enlightened No to something that does not serve your genius, you build a stronger foundation for yourself in the zone.

ANOTHER SHORTCUT: RENEWING
AND REFINING COMMITMENT

Commitment works as a springboard to your Zone of Genius. The moment you make a sincere commitment to living in your Zone of Genius, you propel yourself in that direction. Once you're in the zone, commitment also works magnificently well as a steering mechanism and calibration device to keep you centered there.

Kathlyn and I often say that the art of commitment should really be called the art of recommitment. Commitment gets you started and propels you through the early stages of any game, but it's recommitment that ignites your reserves when you feel like you're going to give up. Those moments of low energy are inevitable (in my experience, at least) when you're on a quest for any worthy goal. The saving move in that moment is to renew your commitment. For example, during the course of your quest you may come up against a deeply buried belief that you are fundamentally unlovable. Those beliefs tend to emerge in the hearts and minds of people as they progress toward permanent occupancy of their Zone of Genius. After all, what ultimate test could we set for ourselves but to mount a search for something we have already decided isn't available anywhere? It's nearly inevitable, then, that you will someday encounter a boulder in the living room of your Zone of Genius. That boulder is the belief that you are unlovable. This false belief fuels a frantic search for something external to yourself that confirms that you are indeed lovable. It's the ultimate trick by that ultimate trickster, your ego, to hold on to its job. It's an issue of job security, and your ego is incredibly dedicated to keeping its job.

Your ego has every right to be scared. It's on notice. In the Zone of Genius, you have no need for your ego. In the Zone of Genius, you don't care about getting approval, getting control, getting even, or any of the other get-oriented goals of the ego. You're a free agent there, ready to respond to the infinite possibilities of the present moment. But when the war erupts between your conviction that love lies outside yourself and the deep knowledge that it's a matter of your own creation, you can feel a kind of cellular exhaustion that seems part of the very cosmos itself. That's when recommitment comes in handy. It's time then to take a deep breath and renew your commitment to living full-time in your Zone of Genius.

Almost on a daily basis I revisit the key commitments of my life in the Zone of Genius. I often speak and think my Ultimate Success Mantra:

I expand in abundance, success, and love every day, as I inspire those around me to do the same.

I move and breathe and hum with the mantra whenever I think of it, and I think of it often. It's become part of the fabric of my being now, as close to me as the feeling of my pulse or the sweet sensation of fresh air in my nostrils. Living in the Zone of Genius is like riding a bicycle. It's not that hard once you get the hang of it. In fact, it's deliciously easy and a source of the onrushing exhilaration that gives human life its best intensity. It exacts a stern requirement, though, that's best not to argue with: you've got to pay exquisite attention. I have a few scars on my hide from not honoring that requirement.

When I hit a wobbly spot on the journey, I seize the moment to make a recommitment. From time to time you will probably lose focus and your attention will wander. It comes with the territory. When it happens, though, it doesn't need to be a big deal. It simply means that you need to recommit to what you've chosen to be here for: expressing your genius in the world in ways that help you and others thrive.

Paying close attention will keep you centered and on track in the Zone of Genius. If you're paying attention, you'll notice when you've slipped out of your commitment to living in your zone. You'll feel off center, perhaps, or nothing will seem to be going right. Then it's time to recommit and keep on moving. There are two high motivations for paying such close attention. First off, it's highly motivating to feel the kind of exhilaration every moment brings you when you're expanding in love, abundance, and success. You're motivated to keep living in the Zone of Genius because it feels so exhilarating. Beyond that, though, there is a special elixir brewed by mixing exhilaration with serenity. The serenity comes from the second part of your Ultimate Success Mantra—to inspire those around you to live in *their* Zone of Genius.

Inspiring others is often touted as a moral imperative, a "should" and a duty, but very few ever speak to the sensual delights of inspiration. One of the most delicious feelings in the world comes from seeing people actually becoming inspired by your commitment to living in your Zone of Genius. Not only is inspiring others good for the others; it feels wonderful to you, too.

Living in Einstein Time

Creating Time for the Full Expression of Your Genius

For your life to work harmoniously, you need to develop a harmonious relationship with time. Most people have a difficult time balancing all of their priorities. And there is no greater priority than transforming your relationship with time. If you get a handle on how time actually operates, your work flows gracefully and at high performance. If you don't, it doesn't. Before I figured out how time actually works, I put in twice as many hours and got half as much done. Everything changed when I figured out the secret of Einstein Time. Now I work half as much and get at least twice as much done. Even though I understand the science behind that shift, it still seems like a miracle to me.

One immediate payoff of getting the correct understanding of time is that you feel less stressed as you go through your day. That's good, but there's an even bigger reward: you free up time for creative thinking. When I give speeches to executive groups such as the Young Presidents Organization, I hear one complaint more than any other: "We don't have time to do the creative thinking that makes the biggest difference in our business." In business as well as life itself, it's easy to get so bogged down in handling details that you don't have time to make new creative breakthroughs. If you put the ideas in this chapter to work for you, you won't have that problem anymore.

When you make the shift to Einstein Time, you experience a major surge in your productivity, creativity, and enjoyment. The shift takes place the moment you embrace one profoundly simple truth:

You're where time comes from.

Embrace and embody this truth, and you can experience a quantum jump in productivity and free time. It works so well it may seem like magic, but it's based on solid science inspired by Einstein's physics.

Once you understand that you're where time comes from, you have the power to make as much of it as you want. You're the boss. I know that might sound strange, but I promise you that this is the way time actually works. Before I started teaching this concept to others, I learned it myself . . . the hard way.

About twenty years ago, in a period of great frustration and stress, I discovered that most of my stress and frustration occurred because I had time all wrong. My conception of time was so skewed that I felt either rushed (not enough time) or bored (too much of it). Most of the time I felt rushed, as if there was never enough time and it was constantly slipping away from me. I never got all the things done that I needed to do, even though I felt like I was working overtime. To escape the distress I was feeling, I took a three-day walkabout in the Rocky Mountain wilderness. I thought that perhaps a few days of dealing with fundamentals such as thunderstorms, pumas, and such would clear my mind.

On the last day of my trip, as I perched on a boulder overlooking a flowing mountain brook, I had a realization that changed my life and gave me my serenity back. I saw that my understanding of time was based on an outmoded, Newtonian paradigm. In that flash of insight I realized that Einstein's paradigm was the way time actually worked. I felt a shift of consciousness inside me. My cells seemed to rearrange themselves around the new understanding. Everything changed in that moment, and from that day until now I've gotten everything done in half the time and have had a great time doing it. As a result, I haven't felt rushed in twenty years. Looked at from the outside, my life is much busier now than when I had my big insight. In spite of that, I never feel hurried.

You don't need a mountain walkabout to bring this awareness into play. After he heard me talk about Einstein Time

at a seminar, a Manhattan stockbroker sent me an e-mail
telling me about what had happened recently on his daily
subway ride to Wall Street. He said that he was running late
one morning and had sprinted to catch the train, trying to
balance a cup of coffee, a bagel, and his briefcase. Jammed
in with the other riders on the crowded train, he started
to look at his watch but couldn't raise his arm because he
was wedged in so tightly between people. He felt a wave of
panic building because he couldn't see what time it was or
assess how late he might be for his meeting. Suddenly he
recalled our conversation about Einstein Time. *Wait a minute,*
he thought, *I am* time, *and I'll make enough of it so I won't be
late for my meeting.* He relaxed his body and tried to focus on
enjoying the moment in spite of his wedged-in state. Since
he didn't have to worry about falling over, he closed his eyes
and put his attention on being just where he was. Soon he
reached his destination and walked out into the crisp morning air. Again he felt the urge to look at his watch, and
again he let the urge pass. When he got to the meeting that
he expected to be late for, nobody was in the room yet. He
sat down alone and relished the at-ease feeling in his body.
Soon people began streaming in, full of complaints about
late trains and buses, slow-moving lines in coffee shops, and
such. He just smiled.

Now I invite you to make the bold move of changing to
Einstein Time. If you're using any time-management system,
put it in a drawer and don't look at it again. In reality, you

probably haven't been using it anyway. Einstein Time is a new kind of time management that reorganizes your conception of time at the very core. It doesn't take any time to use it. In fact, it generates time while also producing abundant rewards in creativity, feelings of ease, and financial well-being.

This new way of being with time delivers four main benefits:

- You get more done in less time.

- You enjoy plenty of time and abundant energy for your most important creative activities.

- You discover your unique abilities and how to express them.

- You feel good inside.

THE PROBLEM

Let's take a close look at the problem that we all face. Along with millions of other busy people, you probably have thought about time quite a bit. You probably have purchased one or more of the time-management systems such as the FranklinCovey system or the one that my neighbor David Allen created. At first you probably had the highest intentions of using it faithfully. However, after the class ended and the consultant departed, you tried to use the system but struggled with its complexity. Eventually, if you used it at all, you kept a small part of it and quit using the rest. You may have even felt guilty that you didn't use it to its full advantage. Then, some time later, you probably bought another one.

I don't want you to feel bad about any of this. You're in good company (mine, for one). Before I figured out the secret of time, I probably studied or bought half a dozen different systems. Give yourself some appreciation for making the noble effort. Your original intention was to solve one of the most difficult problems in modern life: how to get everything done you need to do and still have time for creativity, family, and yourself. This noble intention causes millions of people every year to invest in time-management systems, only to find that they stop using them or that the systems consume more time than they save.

THE SOLUTION

Einstein Time gives you a way to *expand* the amount of time you have for creative expression and intimate connections. With Einstein Time, you not only save time; you'll learn how to become the *source* of time so you can make as much of it as you want. With Einstein Time, you'll also discover how to liberate the energy you need for accomplishing your most precious activities. You'll understand exactly what drains your creative energy and how to stop the drain.

The result: no more rushing, no more time pressure, no more feeling exhausted because you worked all day and didn't get any of the important things done. Instead, you have plenty of time, an abundance of energy, and the skills that will keep both time and energy in a constant state of refreshing renewal.

There is no evidence that the pace of life will become slower in the future. We need ways to organize our time and energy, but the existing systems of time management are useful only up to a point and with certain types of people. For most of us, and especially for creative people, Einstein Time delivers a unique set of benefits. It's simple to understand, easy to implement, and so useful you'll wonder how you ever did without it.

Now it's time to slip out of the time trap you've been caught in so you can soar into the open spaces of your Zone of Genius. While it's possible to make improvements in your work and personal life by applying a Newtonian approach to time, you need to make an Einsteinian shift in order to experience a genuine liberation from time constraints. At best, a Newtonian approach gives us incremental improvements. What we really need, though, is radical transformation. That's where Einstein's paradigm comes into play.

THE OLD PARADIGM

The Newtonian paradigm of time is also its major limitation. The Newtonian view says there's only a finite amount of time, and it must be carefully portioned out so there will be enough of it to do the things we need to do. The Newtonian paradigm assumes that there's a scarcity of time, which leads to an uncomfortable feeling of time urgency inside us. It's exactly the same problem we would have if we assumed there was a scarcity of food. We'd always be hungry, and we'd always be afraid there wasn't enough food available. If you've ever thought that way about time, welcome to a very large club. There's hope, however, because while the Newtonian view is where most of us start, it is not how time actually works. Newtonian time scarcity is just a stage we're passing through, just as Newtonian physics was a stage we passed through on the way to Einstein's breakthrough.

THE NEWTONIAN TIME TRAP IN DETAIL

The Newtonian paradigm guarantees that you will always have a problem with time. You'll either have too little of it or too much. You'll either have "no time at all" or be sitting around with "time on your hands." You'll be rushing to catch up or bored out of your wits. In the Newtonian world, we're either "running out of time" or watching the seconds creep by. Think of how many times in your life you've heard someone say, "I have exactly the right amount of time to enjoy everything I'm doing." I don't believe I've ever heard anybody say anything like that. Most people seem to live at the two extremes of the time continuum: rushing to stay ahead of the clock because they're busy, or virtually brain-dead with boredom because they don't have enough to do.

At the heart of the Newtonian time crunch is a dualistic split: we are deluded into thinking that time is "out there," an actual physical entity that can put pressure on us "in here." That's ridiculous, of course, but try to tell that to a patient in a cardiologist's office. As Meyer Friedman, MD, pointed out in his classic book, *Type A Behavior and Your Heart,* typical heart patients have a marked sense of time urgency. They're in a race with time, and their hearts show the wear and tear of it.

Newtonian dualism pits us against time. In this paradigm, we think of time as the master and us as its slave. At the extreme, time becomes our persecutor, and we think of ourselves as its victim. Since time feels like an ever-present entity hovering in the background of our lives, we come to feel that we're victims of an entity that's always there, all the time. Such a view is dangerous to our health, disastrous for our business, and ruinous to our relationships with family and friends. That's why I urge you to adopt Einstein Time. Not only is it a new paradigm; it can literally be a lifesaver.

OUR TIME PROBLEM: A SPACE PROBLEM

To get to the new, expanded version of time offered by Einstein, we also need to make a few changes in how we think about space. When we're running on Einstein Time, our experience of time changes because we make a fundamental change in how much space we are willing to occupy. By learning to occupy space in a new way, we actually gain the ability to generate more time.

Here's a practical example. Recall Einstein's colloquial explanation of relativity: an hour with your beloved feels like a minute; a minute on a hot stove feels like an hour. This example has everything you need to understand Einstein Time and its powerful positive ramifications for how we live our lives. If you are forced to sit on a hot stove, you become preoccupied with trying *not* to occupy the space you're in. You withdraw your consciousness toward your core, contracting away from the pain of contact with the stove. The act of contracting your awareness away from space makes time congeal. It seems to slow down and harden into a solid mass. The more you cringe from the pain, the slower time gets.

When you're embracing your beloved, though, your awareness flows in the opposite direction, toward space. When you're with your beloved, every cell in your body yearns to be in union with him or her. Your awareness flows out toward your periphery. You want to occupy every possible smidgen of space in the yearned-for present. When you're in love, you relax into the space around you and in you, and as your consciousness expands into space, time disappears. If you even remember to glance at a clock, you notice that time has leaped forward in great spurts. Entire hours can disappear in the wink of an eye. When your heart is beating in time with your beloved's, your every cell is reaching out for total union.

You forget about time. When you're willing to occupy all space, time simply disappears. You're everywhere all at once, there's no place to get to, and everywhere you are it's exactly the right time.

Now, back to the stove. I hope it's been a long time since you've sat on one, so let's use an example that's much more relevant to your daily life. Let's say you notice that your belly muscles are particularly tight on a given morning. You're busy, though, so you don't stop to find out why your stomach's so tight. In other words, you choose not to occupy the space of your tense belly by shining the light of awareness on it. You ignore it and hurry on. This is a costly moment, though, because by choosing not to become aware of why your belly muscles are so tight, you sentence yourself to a daylong battle with time.

Specifically, let's say your belly is tight because you're scared. Let's say you're scared about a visit from your daughter—as recently happened to a friend of mine. He's a single dad whose wife died from cancer several years ago, leaving him with three teenage daughters to raise on his own. Here's the story he told me.

About 9 a.m. I was sitting at my desk working on an article I needed to finish that day. The phone rang; it was my nineteen-year-old daughter, Sara, calling from a phone booth. She said she was on her way home from her college, a six-hour drive away. She told me she needed to talk to me about something important . . . too important to talk about on the phone. My belly clenched into a tight fist when I heard that. I begged her to give me a hint, but she simply said she'd see me in the afternoon. She hung up without even saying good-bye. The conversation was so unlike our usual way of communicating that I was dumbfounded. I actually stood there staring at the phone in my hand for a long moment before I remembered to hang it up. Then I entered a time tunnel for the next six hours. I must have looked at the clock a thousand times. I would try to concentrate on my article, but my mind would wander back to the conversation. Sara had always been the "responsible one," so my mind was jumping through hoops trying to imagine what was going on. Was she pregnant? Had she caught some dread disease? By 3 p.m. my mind felt like it was on the high-speed setting of a Cuisinart. Finally Sara walked in, and I said, *"Where have you been?"* She said she'd stopped for lunch and the restaurant had been jammed. *"Lunch?"* I croaked. The idea of eating during the past seven hours had been unthinkable to me. What had brought her home? She told me that halfway through her school year the full force of grief about her mother's death had descended upon her. She found she didn't want to be there. She wanted to postpone school until the following year, get a temporary job, maybe do some traveling that summer. She was deeply worried that I would feel disappointment and disapproval. She wanted to be able to see my face when she talked to me about the issue. Ten minutes later we were laughing and crying together, best friends again.

He told me that before she walked in the door, time· had seemed "slow as molasses." The minutes crept by, as they will when you look at the clock often. His creative energy disappeared also. No matter how much he tried to busy himself with his work, his mind kept returning to the knot in his belly and the worries in his mind. Suddenly, though, when Sara shared her dilemma and her desires, time took on a different characteristic. An hour or two flew by as they talked about their feelings about her quitting college. Here's the real Einsteinian magic at work, though: when he sat back down to work on his article, his fingers flew over the keyboard, and he finished his project in less than hour. He thought it would take all day to write it, but instead it took a fraction of that time.

THE TRUTH ABOUT TIME AND ALL THE THINGS YOU REALLY DON'T WANT TO DO

You'll never have enough money to buy all the stuff you don't really need, and you'll never have enough time to do all the things you really don't want to do. Our Newtonian concept of both time and money is built on scarcity. The advertising industry thrives on the fact that they know this and most of us don't. Advertising encourages us to want a lot of things we don't really need. It also encourages us to want to do a lot of things we don't really want to do. All those problems disappear on Einstein Time.

To get on Einstein Time, you have to make one big shift, and it's so unthinkable that I've actually heard grown-ups gasp in astonishment when I've suggested they do it. It involves taking full ownership of time. It's such a bold step that very few people have the courage to take it. I'm betting you're one of those few, though.

Stay with me here. The concept is so unusual that it can't be understood in the usual way. We have to peel off layers of old, erroneous programming in order get to the elegant, simple truth of it. One layer that needs to be peeled off is your time persona.

"PARDON ME, MAY I BORROW YOUR PERSONA FOR A MOMENT?"

Part of our problem with time is related to the *persona* we have. A persona is a pattern of actions and feelings that came into being at a certain time in our lives, in response to certain conditions. *Persona*, a Latin word that means "mask," is the root of our more familiar word *personality*. Think back on the different personas you saw around you in your family of origin. The same family can produce one child who wears a Rebel persona, another child with a Mom's Helper persona, and a third with a Class Clown persona. Where and how these personas form is one of the great mysteries that the field of psychology tries to solve. We're going to leave that mystery for the academics, though. Here I want to focus only on the most practical aspect of personas.

WHAT YOU REALLY NEED TO KNOW ABOUT YOUR PERSONA

Everybody's got at least one persona, and most of us have two or three we wear for different occasions. Here's the quirky truth that gets overlooked: most of us probably don't realize that the persona we're wearing is actually a persona. For example, if you've been wearing a Shy Kid persona since you were in kindergarten, as an adult you may actually think you're shy. You may not realize that it's like a suit you put on early in life and have been wearing so long you think it's your skin.

Part of becoming a grown-up is learning to spot when we're operating out of a persona. Part of growing up is discarding the personas that aren't contributing to our happiness and success in life. The Rebel may wake up at age twenty-five and realize that the same amount of effort it takes to rebel against authority can be rechanneled into getting positive attention from authorities. I know. I'm one of them. I got in trouble a lot in high school, college, and elsewhere (often for the antics of my Class Clown persona). I realized in my twenties that much of my Rebel persona came from trying to get attention from male authority figures. I'd grown up without a father, and I believe I hid my grief about that issue under a layer of anger. I took an upside-down approach in my interactions with authority, getting the attention I craved through misbehavior rather than positive contributions. It worked out OK in the long run, because I woke up in time to turn the Rebel energy into creative energy.

Time personas work the same way. Most of us adopt a persona in regard to time, and then we forget it's a persona. We lose sight of the fact that we can take it on and off; it becomes ingrained and semipermanent. Let me give you two examples of time personas from opposite ends of the spectrum. At one end there's the Time Cop, who gets there on time and reminds others to do the same. The Time Cop gets frustrated because people don't show up on time, and gets particularly furious with those folks at the other end of the spectrum, the Time Slackers. If you wear the Time Slacker persona, you're always getting hassled for being late or not showing up at all. If you're a Time Cop, you're often hassling people for not keeping their time agreements.

I will insert a forthright confession here: I'm a Time Cop. This persona has softened a little bit as I've matured, but once a Time Cop, always a Time Cop. I expect that this persona will be with me until my last breath (which will be on time, I can assure you).

I had an employee for a while who was a classic Time Slacker. Wherever she was supposed to be, she was always a little late. Most of the time it didn't cause problems, because her duties around the office were not usually time-sensitive. One time, however, it caused a problem. Her sole duty on a particular day was to pick me up at the airport at a certain time. I got to the curb outside the airport, where she had assured me she would be, and she wasn't there. This was in the era before cell phones were common, so I had no way to find out if she was on her way or had forgotten about it completely. I waited around for a few minutes in the cold, then gave up and got a cab.

Back at the office an hour later she came in and glared at me. "Where were you?" she asked. "I waited at the airport for half an hour!" I could hardly believe my ears. "Where were *you?*" I asked. "I stood around waiting for ten minutes, then took a twenty-five-dollar cab ride home." She gave me a classic Time Slacker answer. "I was only fifteen minutes late," she said, delivering this line with a tone of exasperated victimhood. I asked her, "How was I supposed to know you were only going to be fifteen minutes late? For all I knew, you'd forgotten about it completely." She rolled her eyes, as in "How can you possibly be so uptight?"

It was a clash of the time personas: my Time Cop versus her Time Slacker. In this case, the Time Cop was the one who was providing the paychecks, so my persona carried the day. Two little words suggested themselves to me. I paused to roll them around in my mind, savoring their sweetness, and then spoke them to her: "You're fired." She was liberated from the bonds of my Time Cop persona, free to go slack on somebody else.

EINSTEIN TIME

When we switch to Einstein Time, we take charge of the amount of time we have. We realize that we're where time comes from. We embrace this liberating insight: *since I'm the producer of time, I can make as much of it as I need!* By getting the truth of this statement, we make a major adjustment in ourselves. We heal the dualistic split embedded in the Newtonian relationship with time. We are no longer in an us-versus-them relationship with time. We're the source of time, and by realizing that fact we become the truth of it.

It takes practice and keen awareness to master this concept. I'll show you how to make the most of your practice and what to focus your awareness on. If all this sounds mysterious and elusive, just remember: so did driving a car before you could do it. When I first sat in the driver's seat as a kid, I was sure I could never figure out all those complicated moves. I did, though, and you did, too. If you can do that, you can master Einstein Time. It's like driving, but with no car.

I'll be blunt here, just as blunt as when I'm confronting limitations in my own mind: Quit thinking time is "out there." Take ownership of time—acknowledge that you are where it comes from—and it will stop owning you. Claim time as yours, and it will release its claim on you. The best way I've found to do that is to become nimble at asking a specific question. The question allows you to seize the controls of your time and your life.

There's no trick to the process. You could probably take ownership of time without the question, simply by claiming time as yours to invent as you wish. You could do it by saying something to yourself like "I acknowledge that I'm the source of time." Look in the mirror and say, "I'm where time comes from." Or, if you're one of those folks who like to lecture themselves sternly, say, "There's no such thing as time 'out there,' meathead. It all comes from inside you. You are *not* time's victim!" However, the question makes it simple and easy.

To generate an abundance of time, ask yourself,

Where in my life am I not taking full ownership?

Another way to ask it is:

What am I trying to disown?

Or:

What aspect of my life do I need to take full ownership of?

The answer is always blindingly obvious, but we can't see it until we get humble enough to ask the question. Here's the principle behind the question: stress and conflict are caused by *resisting* acceptance and ownership. If there is any part of ourselves or our lives that we're not fully willing to accept, we will experience stress and friction in that area. The stress will disappear the moment we accept that part and claim ownership of it. At that moment, the disowned part of us is embraced into the wholeness of ourselves, and from that place of wholeness, miracles are born.

For example, if one of your children has a drug problem, you will experience more and more stress and conflict the longer you deny ownership of the problem. If you refuse to look at the problem, your denial will produce greater stress and conflict. If you look at the problem but transfer ownership by saying, "This isn't my problem; this is my child's problem," you will experience more stress and conflict. Resolution of the problem will begin the moment you or the child claims ownership. It is important to note that one person usually claims ownership first. In my experience, it is rare for both people to step into responsibility at the same time. If you claim ownership first, full resolution won't occur until your child also claims ownership. When both of you decide to take ownership, as in "This is my problem and I'm committed to resolving it," you can work genuine miracles. I've seen such miracles hundreds of times.

HOW TO BEGIN

Begin with time itself. Do whatever it takes to get yourself in harmony with the reality that you're the *source* of time. Once you're convinced, start acting as if it's true. A simple way to begin is to put yourself on a radical diet: complete abstinence from complaining about time. This courageous move will take you out of the victim position in regard to time. When you stop complaining about time, you cease perpetuating the destructive myth that time is the persecutor and you are its victim. I found this surprisingly hard when I first started the diet. Until I went on the diet, I hadn't realized how many of my conversations contained complaints about time. Notice the conversations around you this week. See how many times you hear things like:

"I wish I had time to stop and chat, but I'm in a hurry."

"Where did the time go?"

"There simply aren't enough hours in the day."

"If only I'd gotten another hour of sleep."

"Love to talk but I've gotta run . . ."

"I have to get to the bank . . ."

"I don't have time to do that right now."

Each of those statements contains an overt or covert complaint, portraying the speaker as a victim of time. It treats time as a scarce commodity, sending the message that time is "out there" and that there isn't enough of it "in here." Each statement is a miniwhimper of misery, a claim that time is the whip master and we're its hapless galley slaves, rowing desperately to stay ahead of the lash. The moment you stop complaining about time, you free up the necessary energy to mount a similar campaign on the inner plane. You will need that energy, because it is one thing to stop complaining that you are the victim of time, but it is quite another to stop *feeling* that you're its victim.

One particular phrase I'd like you to eliminate is this common one: *I don't have time to do that right now.* Like many of us, you probably use it often. Based on what you've learned in this chapter, you can probably now see that it's a lie. It's a lie for two reasons: First, time is not something you have or don't have. You're the source of it, and you make as much of it as you want. Second, when you say, "I don't have time to do that right now," you're telling a polite lie to avoid saying, "I don't want to do that right now." By placing the blame on time, you avoid confronting the blunt truth of the matter.

Imagine that you have an eight-year-old child who comes in while you're working on something and says, "Will you play catch with me?" You reply, "I don't have time to do that right now." Imagine, though, that the child comes in and says, "I just stepped on a nail and my foot is bleeding. Can you help me?" You probably wouldn't say, "I don't have time to do that right now." In actuality, you have exactly the same amount of time as when you used the excuse of lack of time to avoid playing catch. The truth of the matter is that you *didn't* want to play catch and you *do* want to stop the bleeding. By using time as the culprit, you place yourself in the victim position once again. You did it to be polite. (By the way, I'm not advocating that you be blunt with anyone, especially eight-year-old children. I'm advocating that you stop using time or lack of time as an excuse. It's just as polite to say to your child, "I want to finish what I'm working on before I play catch," rather than claiming to be the victim of time.)

THE SENSATION OF TIME PRESSURE

Notice what time pressure feels like in your body. Think of it as another sensation like hunger. We usually register hunger as gnawing, unpleasant contractions in the middle of the front of our bodies. What does time pressure feel like in your body? What does being in a hurry feel like? What does the sluggish side of the time continuum—the sensation most people call "boredom"—feel like to you?

In me, the pressure of being in a hurry feels like pressure between my spine and my heart, pushing toward the front of my chest. Your sensation might be different, or it might be similar to mine. When I tune in to time pressure, I also feel neck tension and the sensation that I'm pushing slightly forward with my head. That's me in a hurry. The other end of the continuum—boredom—feels like a deadened, shadowy darkness in the front of my chest, running from my collarbone down to my navel. As I tune in to those sensations right this moment, I realize that I much prefer being in a hurry to being bored. If I had to pick one, there'd be no choice. It occurs to me that I've organized much of my life to avoid the possibility of being bored.

As I tune in to the "being in a hurry" feeling in my body, I feel the surge of another awareness. I realize it's not being in a hurry that is the real source of the feeling; it's the feeling of creative ferment happening inside me. I love the slightly chaotic inner feeling of having a bunch of interesting things to find out, of asking big questions and waiting for answers to appear, of not quite having figured out things I'm passionately interested in. That's when I feel most alive, and I like having that feeling of aliveness all the time.

As a result, I can remember only one instance of being bored in the past thirty years. My instance of boredom came about because I decided to retire when I was fifty. I saw myself going on leisurely beach strolls with my wife, writing the occasional haiku, living off book royalties, and tugging thoughtfully at the beard I had always intended to grow. My wife vividly remembers my retirement, too, because she still talks about it as the longest three weeks of her life. I turned out to be an utter failure at retirement. I took plenty of leisurely beach strolls with Kathlyn, and I think I even wrote a haiku or two. One day in the third week of my retirement, I was out on a beach walk when an unexpected thought crept into my mind: *I'm bored.*

It wasn't that I missed being in a hurry; I just realized that my very nature is saturated with an urge to be creating something all the time, and preferably three or four things at the same time. That's when I feel most alive. So, I said farewell to retirement and have been happily in ferment ever since.

After seeing the powerful results of my "no complaints about time" diet, I started inviting my clients to put themselves on it. They harvested remarkable results, too.

Here are some of the benefits they told me about:

"We found ourselves getting more things done without feeling rushed."

"We ended the workday feeling less fatigue."

"We suddenly had time to carry out leisurely conversations that we would have cut short in times past."

One of my clients, an executive in a talent agency, gave a particularly good example of the changes he experienced:

I would compare it to changing from using my elbows to drive a car to realizing I could use my hands. Suddenly a lot of frantic activity seemed no longer necessary. Before I took responsibility for the amount of time I had at my disposal, I felt I was in an ongoing wrestling match with time. I saw time as a big, threatening pressure that was always about to overwhelm me. When I learned the real truth—that I'm the source of both the time and the pressure—it was like a huge weight lifted off me.

That's exactly what it feels like.

AN INVITATION

At this point it would be traditional for me to say something like "Take plenty of time to master these principles." However, since you are the source of time, we will amend that to "*Make* plenty of time to master these principles."

The original insight—that we are the source of time, that time is not a pressure from outside, that we can make as much as we need—takes only a split second to comprehend. However, it takes a lot of practice to integrate that insight into the practicalities of our lives. The main thing it takes is keen attention. Be on the lookout constantly for complaints about time that come out of your mouth or go through your mind. As you spot them and eliminate them one by one, you will grow steadily less busy while getting a great deal more done.

Now I'll step aside and let you take charge. I've told you everything I know about Einstein Time, and you have everything you need to know to implement it. Let the good times roll.

SEVEN

Solving the Relationship Problem

Transcending the Upper Limits of Love and Appreciation

As you know by now, the essential move we all need to master is learning to handle more positive energy, success, and love. Instead of focusing on the past, we need to increase our tolerance for things going well in our lives *now*. If we don't learn how to do this, we suffer in every area of our lives. One area that suffers spectacularly is our relationships. As we bump into our Upper Limit Problems, relationships are one of the key areas that suffer greatly. In fact, the greater success you achieve, the bumpier your relationships tend to be. I'll explain why and show you how to avoid this last pervasive barrier.

John Cuber and Peggy Harroff conducted one of the few in-depth studies ever done on the relationships of successful people. The authors found that 80 percent of the 437 successful people they studied had unsatisfying marriages and long-term relationships. Only about 20 percent of the couples had relationships the authors called *vital*. The other 80 percent had three main styles of unsatisfying relationships:

1. In *devitalized* relationships, the partners remained together in spite of having fallen out of love with each other years ago. They had been "going through the motions," sometimes for decades. The relationships often looked OK from the outside, but there was little or no passion between the individuals.

2. In *passive-congenial* relationships, the partners had never been passionate about each other in the first place. Their relationship was based more on affectionate friendship; they were much like business partners. Their expectations were low, so they were seldom disappointed with each other. Because of the low expectations, they didn't fight much and so remained together in a state of ho-hum harmony.

3. In *conflict-habituated* relationships, the partners had created a lifestyle based around constant conflict. Whether engaged in low-level bickering or heated conflict, they remained in long-term combat

interrupted by periods of truce. They seemed almost
to thrive on conflict, which provided them with an
adrenaline-infused state of ongoing arousal.

I felt a wave of despair when I first saw these findings. If
these highly successful people had such dismal relationships,
was there any hope for the rest of us? It's been twenty years
since I first saw this study, and with those years has come
considerable experience working with people and their relationships. I don't think the overall statistics are any different
now than when Cuber and Harroff first published their results. In other words, I think the majority of successful people
still have dismal relationships. Now, though, I know a lot
more about how they got that way. More important, I know a
lot more about how they can avoid falling into the traps that
many successful people get stuck in. I feel a great deal more
hope now than I did twenty years ago. The reason is that I've
seen many successful people transform their relationships—
whether devitalized, conflict-habituated, or passive-congenial—into vital unions.

There are two main reasons that successful people have
dismal relationships: (1) simply because they're successful;
and (2) because they don't know how the Upper Limit Problem works. The very fact of being successful makes it more
likely that the relationship will be troubled, because both
partners have to deal with the Upper Limit Problem to a more
intense degree. Let me give you an example.

I worked with a famous couple that would definitely fit the conflict-habituated category. To safeguard their privacy, I'll call them Jim and Jane. Things had been going quite well in their relationship during the first five years, but a sudden upsurge of success tripped their Upper Limit switch. Suddenly they were on the covers of magazines, and ultimately they even attracted ugly badges of success such as paparazzi and stalkers. By the time they got to me, they had been bickering and arguing for nearly two years straight.

Recall that one of the biggest drivers of the Upper Limit Problem is a false belief that says, "I'm fundamentally flawed and don't deserve success." This false belief dominated their early lives, although neither of them recognized it until they gained an understanding of the Upper Limit Problem. When I explained to them how the ULP worked, and how old beliefs spring forth to pull us back down into the old familiar negative sense of ourselves, their famous faces actually paled in recognition.

Mine did, too, when it first dawned on me how much I was sabotaging my own efforts to get the love I so craved. Fortunately, I made some of these discoveries before I met Kathlyn in 1980, so I didn't have to use our relationship as the laboratory for all of my early experiments. By the time I met her, I had seen the destructive power of my own barriers to giving and receiving love. Particularly, I had seen the power of projection, a subject that in my opinion should be in the curriculum of all elementary schools everywhere.

A vast amount of energy can be liberated in relationships by dropping the habit of projection. As mentioned, projection occurs when you attribute to others something that's true for you inside yourself. For example, a man may complain to me that his wife is too passive. If he were to own the projection, he would say, "I have not learned to handle a relationship in which a woman is being powerful and equal, so I create relationships with women in which I require them to be passive." A woman may complain that her partner dominates her and limits her full expression. If she were to own the projection, she would say, "I attract men who dominate and control me. I have not learned how to be my own boss and take up my full space in the world."

Projection is the source of power struggles that eat up energy and intimacy in relationships. Power struggles are a war between two people to see whose version of reality will win out. Much of the energy in troubled relationships is drained through power struggles about who's right, who's wrong, and who's the biggest victim. Relationships—healthy ones, that is—exist only between equals. When both people are not taking 100 percent responsibility, it is an entanglement, not a relationship. There is only one way to transform an entanglement into a relationship: both people must drop projection and see that they are 100 percent the creators of their reality. With the energy saved from banishing power struggles, much more can be co-created than the partners could have created on their own.

If both people in a relationship can understand the Upper Limit Problem, they can begin to adjust the thermostat upward so they can handle increasingly more positive energy. The thermostat can be adjusted upward in several ways. Just noticing how you limit love and positive energy solves much of the problem. Do you bring yourself down with food? Do you drink too much? Do you deflect compliments? Do you find yourself thinking of something else while making love? Do you get sick the day of an opportunity for intimacy in the relationship? Do you hold back on communicating instead of reaching out to people?

The Upper Limit Problem is magnified in successful couples, because each person is synergizing the other's quest for a life in the Zone of Genius. At the same time, though, they are synergizing each other's tendencies toward self-sabotage. Couples who wish to transcend these tendencies will benefit from making a mutual commitment to transcending Upper Limits and living with each other in the Zone of Genius. If both people are committed to getting there, the journey becomes much easier.

In any case, it's a heroic task. The reason is twofold: because most of us have little experience observing healthy relationships; and because having healthy relationships is a new task in evolution. For the first couple of million years of human evolution, relationships were about survival, and communication was largely a matter of exchanging grunts. We're newcomers to the idea of having our relationships be about fulfillment, heartfelt communications, and deep commitment to each other. Any of us who embark on a path of conscious growth must remember that we're bringing with us millions of years of evolution. There is no quicker way to bring forth our inner Neanderthal than to get into a loving relationship. When we open up to more love and energy, we begin to flush old programming out of our system. Our energy thermostat is reset higher, and sometimes this sets off alarms in ourselves. Genuine contact with another person gets us high, and this trips the Upper Limit switch, making us want to come back down to a more familiar level.

There are several ways we limit positive energy in relationships. One is by starting arguments, out of fear of intimacy, at times when we could be exchanging intimacy. Another is by withholding significant communications. We get scared of being close, for example, and instead of telling the microscopic truth about it ("My belly felt tight and my skin contracted when I heard you say . . ."), we withdraw and swallow the communication. Another way we limit positive energy is by needing to control or dominate the other person (or needing to be controlled or dominated). If we always have to be right, for example, there is no room in the relationship to be happy.

If you're a successful person in a close relationship, you will likely find the following suggestions helpful.

1. Make sure you take plenty of time for yourself, in a space apart from your partner. It could even be in the

next room, so long as the intention is to nurture the independent part of you. Human beings have twin drives of equal power: the urge to merge and the urge to be an autonomous person. For a relationship to thrive, both drives need to be celebrated.

A close relationship stirs up powerful transformative energies, and you need lots of rest time to integrate the rapid-fire stimulation that a relationship provides. If you can learn to take time off from the relationship consciously, you won't need to do it unconsciously by starting arguments and engaging in other intimacy-destroying moves. Go on solo walks, take in a movie by yourself, spend an afternoon doing whatever the spirit moves you to do. These periods of battery-charging alone time give you the ability to master longer and longer periods of closeness when you're in union with your beloved.

2. Put a priority on speaking the microscopic truth, especially about what is going on in your emotions. Get skilled at simple microscopic truths such as "I'm sad," "I'm scared," and "I feel angry." Communicating about feelings, dreams, desires, and other inner experiences creates deep intimacy in relationships. None of us gets any training in how to communicate about these simple things, and our lack of training is very costly.

3. When emotions are in the air, as they often will be in close relationships, don't try to talk yourself or your partner out of them. Eliminate phrases such as "Please don't cry" and "There's nothing to be angry about." Feelings are to be felt, so encourage each other to go through complete cycles of emotions. If you're sad, let yourself feel that way until you don't feel sad anymore. Same thing with fear, anger, happiness, and other feelings. It's the act of stifling and concealing feelings that causes problems in relationships.

4. Give yourself and your partner plenty of nonsexual touch. Sexual touch is great, but humans need nonsexual touch in large quantities. A loving hand squeeze or a touch on the shoulder communicates love and caring in ways no words can.

5. After soaring to a new height of intense intimacy, bring yourself back to ground in a positive way. Many people, when they enjoy a time of deep closeness, unconsciously create an argument or accident to get their feet back on the ground. It's not necessary to use a painful method of grounding yourself. It works much better, and is much more fun, to come back to earth by doing some earthy dancing, taking a walk on the surface of the earth, or cleaning out a closet full of your earthly possessions.

6. Cultivate at least three friends with whom you can form a No-Upper-Limits conspiracy. The word *conspiracy* comes from two Latin roots that together mean "to breathe together." That's the kind of conspiracy I want you to create. I want you to feel the power of two or more people in harmony, working toward a benign goal that's good for all. You and the other members of your conspiracy will educate each other on the Upper Limit Problem. You will spot each other running Upper Limit behaviors such as worrying, getting sick, having accidents, and so forth. You and your conspiracy will gently remind each other that you create the quality of your life experience out of your beliefs. You'll remind each other to examine those beliefs to make sure they're giving you room for ultimate success in love and life. When you trip and fall, as we all tend to do from time to time, you and your co-conspirators will remind each other to take a deep breath, center yourselves, and open up again to feeling more love, abundance, and success than you've ever before enjoyed.

If you're a successful person in relationship with another successful person, you've embarked on one of the great quests in all human endeavor. For me, it's the ultimate thrill ride, a journey in which every moment is packed with learning potential and the opportunity to experience true joy.

With the ideas and tools we've explored in this book, you have everything you need to set sail and navigate the tricky swirls and currents of intimate relationships. The rest is practice. No matter how brilliant we might be at making money or making music or making soup, we are all amateurs when it comes to feeling and expressing love. I like it that way, because it gives every moment of life an exhilarating learning edge. It keeps me cheerfully humble to think of myself as a beginner in a field in which I'm acclaimed as an expert. I also know, from painful experience, that the moment my attitude of cheerful humility slips into self-righteousness or arrogance, the universe will just as cheerfully step in with an unexpected way to make me humble again. The universe will teach us our lessons with the tickle of a feather or the whomp of a sledge-hammer, depending on how open we are to learning the particular lesson. Getting stubborn and defensive invites the sledgehammer; getting open and curious invites the feather. It took me a long time to figure out who was in charge of the painfulness of my lessons.

To prevent humiliating collisions with the universe, I suggest we all adopt an attitude of being open to learning in every moment of our relationships. Every interaction contains within it the possibility of deep connection with our beloved, with ourselves, and with the cosmos. Relationship is the ultimate spiritual path, because it constantly presents us with the challenge to love and embrace in the very situations in which we're most prone to shun and reject. For that reason above all, relationship is the place where our spirituality most visibly comes to light. You can tell more about a person's true spirituality from the way he or she treats his or her partner than you ever could from tallying that person's church attendance.

The key to spiritual development through relationship is being open to learning from every moment of interaction. By doing so, we welcome the ups and downs of relationship instead of resisting them. We approach each moment with an open mind and a willing heart. This attitude cuts down on friction, enhances the possibility of deep connection, and keeps us from being battered when turbulence occurs.

In that spirit, let me close our discussion of successful people and relationships with a translation I made of a poem by the fourteenth-century mystic Hafiz.

YOUR DIVINE INVITATION

You're invited to meet the Divine.
Nobody can resist an invitation like that!

Now, your choices narrow to two:
You can come to the Divine ready to dance.
Or
Be carried on a stretcher to the Divine Emergency Room.

Conclusion

As you move toward greater success, love, abundance, and creativity in your life, you will encounter the Upper Limit Problem. I say it is the only problem you really need to solve. The problem, though challenging, brings a priceless gift hidden within it. The gift reveals itself as you explore and solve the problem. The gift is a special kind of relationship: a living connection with the source of genius within you.

The Upper Limit Problem is our universal human tendency to sabotage ourselves when we have exceeded the artificial upper limit we have placed on ourselves. The Upper Limit Problem is caused by a too-low thermostat setting on our ability to achieve and enjoy our ultimate success. The thermostat gets set low early in our lives, at a time when we could not think for ourselves. Later, as we dream about big goals and move up into realms of love, abundance, and creativity that are above our old thermostat setting, we bump up against the artificial lid that was placed on our success through unconscious childhood decisions. Unless we solve the Upper Limit

Problem, we will keep finding ways to bring ourselves back down when we've blown past our old setting.

The childhood decisions all were made unconsciously as we navigated through difficult family crosscurrents. Those unconscious decisions become barriers we must overcome in order to express and enjoy our full measure of success. There are four of these barriers:

The first barrier is the false belief that we are fundamentally flawed in some way. If we carry this feeling within us, we sabotage our success because we think we're essentially bad. If something good happens, we must mess up to offset it, because good things can't happen to bad people.

The second barrier is the false belief that by succeeding, we are being disloyal to and leaving behind people in our past. If we harbor this feeling within us, we sabotage our success because we think it's disloyal to our roots to soar too far into the stratosphere.

The third barrier is the false belief that we are a burden in the world. If we carry this feeling inside us, we sabotage our success so that we won't be a bigger burden.

The fourth barrier is the false belief that we must dim the bright lights of our brilliance so that we won't outshine someone in our past. If we hold this feeling inside us, we tend to hold ourselves back from expressing the full potential of our innate genius.

Understanding why we've limited ourselves liberates a new energy in us, which we can draw on to propel us to new heights of abundance, love, and creativity. As we spiral upward in our quest to express our unique genius, we will likely soar past ghosts and shadows of those old barriers. For this reason, it's best to think of our quest as a continuing journey of transcending upper limits. The payoff for the work is a gift of enduring value: we get to live in the full rainbow of our potential, in our Zone of Genius. In that exalted space, we enjoy the love, abundance, and success we create, and our very presence inspires people wherever we go in the world.

We transcend our Upper Limit Problem each time we make more room inside us to feel more love, abundance, and success. It's done moment by moment, and the moment goes like this: We catch ourselves worrying or starting an argument. Suddenly we realize we're Upper-Limiting. We let go of the train of worry-thoughts or the huffy point of view, taking a deep breath or two for relaxation. Perhaps we wiggle our toes or stretch our shoulders in a gesture of opening up space to feel more love, success, and abundance. A moment later we break free of the Upper Limit and feel a flow of good feeling again. In wink-of-an-eye moments such as these, we expand our capacity to enjoy more love, abundance, and success.

These moments are the springboards of our Big Leap. It may not happen in our first moment or our hundred-and-first, but if we practice with diligence and zeal, one magic day we will look up and realize we have created our beautiful life in the Zone of Genius. On that day we will look around us and see other friendly faces in their Zone of Genius. We'll look at each other and say, "Welcome, friend." On that day we'll know that heaven and earth are truly one.

As you and I come to the end of our time together in this book, I want to tell you how grateful I am to be sharing these ideas and processes with you. They are sacred treasures to me, and I feel blessed to have been entrusted with them. I feel doubly blessed for a lifetime of teaching them to others. The experience of learning what is in these pages has gifted me with a life of more magnificence than I ever knew existed; passing them along to you has allowed me to fulfill my life's grandest purpose. For that great privilege, I thank you from the top, middle, and bottom of my heart.

As my work on this book was drawing to a close, I went out into the backyard to stretch my legs and get some fresh air. It was approaching dusk, and the blossoms of evening were just beginning to breathe their fragrance into the air. I sat for a few minutes in our swing, enjoying the soft breezes, the sweet air, and the sounds of my neighborhood. I could see Kathlyn in the living room, deep in communion with a novel by one of her favorite mystery writers. I could feel a warm, glad-to-be-home sensation within me, and as I expanded my attention to let myself enjoy it thoroughly, waves of bliss spread through me. Suddenly my mind chimed in with a philosophical observation: "This won't last forever, but it's wonderful while it's happening." I realized with a chuckle that this commentary, whether wise or trite, was a subtle Upper Limit behavior. I had obviously exceeded my tolerance for backyard bliss. My Old Philosopher persona had shuffled in from the shadows to bring me back to earth. I gave the old fellow a loving pat on the back and sent him back to his quiet corner. Then I turned my attention back to where it belongs: feeling the blissful richness of this fine moment.

Here is my wish for you: a life journey blessed with many such moments of discovery. Going forward on your path, may your every day be filled with much practical magic and many everyday miracles. May you transcend each and every one of your upper limits, and long may you glide the high currents of love, abundance, and creative contribution.

Baby Steps and Big Leaps
My Early Adventures
As an Entrepreneur

When I give talks to business audiences such as the Young Presidents Organization, I notice that the entrepreneurs in the audience often show the most enthusiasm for my ideas. I feel a natural resonance with entrepreneurs, partly because I've been having entrepreneurial adventures since I was a kid. I've also found that entrepreneurs are often most receptive to one of my core beliefs: that business is ultimately a spiritual path.

I've found that business and every other aspect of life goes much better if I stay in touch with the spiritual aspect of myself. There's a good reason for this: if I make a split between money and spirituality, as I did for part of my life, I cannot harness the most awesome power we have, our spiritual essence. If we can heal that split and realize that money is simply spiritual energy in motion, we can put the power of spirit to work for us in creating wealth with ease and flow.

I had a personal experience early in my life that left an enduring impression on me. It was the first spiritual experience I can clearly remember, and it happened when I was five years old, the summer before I was in elementary school. I was playing by myself in the side yard on a hot summer day in Florida. I had just come home from spending a morning in a children's program at my family's church. The program featured stories of Jesus, art projects involving Jesus, and songs of the "Jesus Loves Me" variety. There was great emphasis on Jesus's role as the Son of God.

As I played outside, I was thinking about the Son of God part of the story. What did this mean exactly? I had never known a living father, because he had died during my mother's pregnancy with me. I didn't have any felt-sense of what it might feel like to have a father. Suddenly I found myself wondering if I, too, was a Son of God. It seemed that if Jesus could be the Son of God, maybe I could be, too.

This thought sent a thrill through me, a wave of exhilarating feeling I can remember as vividly as if it happened a minute ago. I looked up through the branches of the trees into the blue sky shimmering in the tropical air. Is that where my father lives? Is that where I came from?

Then a special kind of awareness settled into me, a sure knowledge that seemed so obvious I wondered why I hadn't thought of it before: I am made of the same stuff as everything else. The trees, the sky, the earth beneath me—we're all made of the same thing and it is all one thing. Everything is connected to everything else. I am the Son of God and everyone else is, too. It has to be that way, because everything is connected and everything is equal.

I remember lying on my back looking up through the trees for a long time. A feeling of deep peace and contentment settled into me. The feeling continued for hours, even after I tried to describe my experience at dinner (and got a few blank stares of the "What the heck are you talking about?" variety). Somehow it didn't matter whether people understood, though, because I knew what I felt and I felt what I knew.

Later in life I came across a stunning passage from *The Meditations of Marcus Aurelius,* which spoke directly to me across time from first-century Rome:

> I am part of the whole, all of which is governed by nature.
> . . . I am intimately related to all the parts, which are of
> the same kind as myself. If I remember these two things,
> I cannot be discontented with anything that arises out of
> the whole, because I am connected to the whole.

A Roman emperor would seem to have little in common with a kid in a sleepy southern town. Somehow, though, the same awareness showed up in both of us. Why and how could that be? After wondering about those questions for many years, I've now become convinced that we eventually become aware of our unity with the whole because it's inescapable. The awareness is wired into us, because we're wired into the universe. We can try with all our might to pretend we're separate from the rest of the universe, but one way or the other it will catch up to us and welcome us back into its embrace.

ENTREPRENEURIAL BABY STEPS

It must have been around that time that I hatched my first entrepreneurial venture. It was an utter failure, at least in the traditional sense, because I didn't attract a single customer. However, it foretold with uncanny accuracy my ultimate career and also illustrated several of the key spiritual principles I've drawn on ever since. [The following is an extended version of one of the stories that appears in the book.]

You've heard of "outside the box" thinking? Well, my first business was literally "inside the box." With Granddad's help, I cut a door in the side of a large cardboard box, which I installed in a corner of my grandparents' living room. This became my office. Above the door was the word *Problems,* which I hand-lettered in red (assisted in spelling by Granddad). I commuted to work on my tricycle, parked it next to the box, and clambered inside to work with my clients.

I had a tough time explaining to my family the exact nature of the business I was in. I made it clear to the family that I did not handle medical problems. They could go to a "regular" doctor for that sort of thing. I explained as best I could that I handled problems you didn't take to a regular doctor, like how to get along better with other people. I was in the people-fixing business, with the stated goal of helping people be happy. To appreciate the unlikelihood of my chosen job, you should know that I grew up in a small town in Florida that had no psychiatrists or psychologists or any other kind of mental health professional. It's a mystery to me where I might have gotten the idea to be a "Problems" doctor.

Although my family of lovable lunatics certainly could have used my services, none of them ever climbed into the box with me. I was forced to work with imaginary patients, whom I cured of everything from general misery to specific ailments. The only specific ailment I can remember at the moment is that I cured one imaginary patient of the tendency to bark like a dog. My family found all this endlessly amusing, and were still telling stories about it well into my adulthood. (By the way, if you're thinking I've got a great memory, I don't. However, I was blessed with a journalist for a mother. Mom wrote a column every day for the local paper, and my adventures often served as material for her column. Thankfully she clipped and saved hundreds of her columns, which have proven to be worth gold in refreshing my memory of my childhood enthusiasms.)

THE JOY OF THE ENTREPRENEUR: CREATING

The ultimate joy of being an entrepreneur is creating something that people find valuable, particularly if it's something that hasn't existed before. My cardboard box counseling center was not valued by the customers, but nothing like it had ever existed before, at least in the part of the world I lived in. To this day, few things give me more satisfaction than inventing something that hasn't existed before. Many of my inventions have been total failures in the financial sense, while others have gone on to make millions of dollars. In the larger sense, all of them have been winners, because they held the fascination of creating something from nothing.

MY BRIEF CAREER IN THE EGG BUSINESS

I hatched an egg business when I was in the second grade. It was my second entrepreneurial attempt, and it ended in a disaster reminiscent of Humpty-Dumpty. My mother financed some chickens for me; the plan was that I would pay her back through the sale of the eggs, hand-delivered to neighbors, then go on to reap vast profits in the egg business.

I underestimated the amount of daily work it took to feed and maintain my chickens, but other than that the plan began to pay off. My chickens began to lay eggs, and all went well for the first few deliveries. One day I was rushing to make a delivery when I tripped climbing the steps of Mr. and Mrs. Geiger's house. I landed on top of the dozen eggs I was carrying, wiping out my profits for the entire week.

Not long after that, I faced another disaster: my chickens escaped, causing me to spend a hot afternoon rounding them up from the neighborhood. Unbeknownst to me, during their break for liberation some of the chickens had feasted on camphor berries from a neighbor's tree. My next batch of eggs tasted and smelled like Vick's Vapo-Rub. The end of my egg career was near. My mother began having second thoughts about the egg business. She was under pressure from the neighbors, who didn't like the racket the chickens made in the backyard. Finally she shut my operation down, with very little complaint from me, and we donated the chickens to a farmer we knew.

I looked for other business opportunities, and soon spotted an opportunity that had all the ingredients of a winning enterprise. I would soon learn, though, something quite contrary to an old saying.

WHEN LIFE GIVES YOU LEMONS, DON'T MAKE LEMONADE!

When I was nine years old I launched a lemonade stand, which quickly taught me the truth of the old saying "location is everything." I moved it to four different corners of my block before finding the one with the most foot traffic. I also learned a few other key truths on my first day of business:

- Flies love lemonade.

- Ice melts fast in Central Florida.

- You have to stand around shooing flies a long time in order to sell a pitcher of lemonade.

According to the family story, though, there was another problem: I drank up a lot of my profits. I've conveniently forgotten this part of the story, but I suspect there may be some truth in it. If you stand around a pitcher of cold lemonade for long enough on a hot day, you're going to want to take a swig.

After a few days in the lemonade business, I decided to fold the enterprise and seek my fortune somewhere else.

Finally, though, I found a business that worked, and made my first dollar as a professional entrepreneur. The difference between an amateur and a professional is very simple: $1. The moment you make a buck of "keeping money" from your entrepreneurial efforts you're a professional, and I attained professional status when I was ten years old.

BREAKTHROUGH!

It was the summer after fifth grade when I conceived my first successful business. I also learned something incredibly useful for any business enterprise: think from the customer's point of view. My next-door neighbor, Mr. Lewin, was in the watermelon and Christmas tree business. An odd combination, you might think, but not for a guy who liked to spend half the year in Florida and half the year in Long Island. While he was in Florida for the winter, he shipped watermelons northward. While he was in Long Island for the summer, he made deals that would ship the trees south to Florida the next winter.

I admired Sam Lewin for lots of things. First of all, he was a great source of stories, having walked across Russia to escape Cossacks. He settled in Germany, only to encounter more intolerant types there. I loved talking to a man who had dealt with real-life Cossacks and Nazis; who spoke Yiddish, German, and Russian; and who could talk into two telephones at once. Mr. Lewin would put one phone down into his lap, fire off a burst of Yiddish into the other phone, then switch back to English on the first phone. By hanging around Mr. Lewin, I collected a great arsenal of Yiddish words and phrases I used when I wanted to hurl innovative insults at my friends. If I remember correctly, *gonif* (thief) and *schlemiel* (habitual screwup) were a couple of my favorite epithets. In my neighborhood there were copious opportunities to use both of these terms.

I came up with the idea of selling watermelons by the side of the highway that ran through my hometown. This was long before Interstate 95, the big freeway that now runs through Florida. In my day southbound motorists had to percolate through the many small towns of Highway 27. Each town had its own speed trap (and rumor had it that my little town made much of its annual budget from nabbing Northerners speeding toward Miami.) For a watermelon entrepreneur, this was a dream come true. My watermelon location had a stream of hot drivers poking along at the local speed limit of twenty-five miles per hour.

Mr. Lewin fronted me four watermelons to sell, and I agreed to split the profits with him. In those days whole watermelons sold for about twenty-five cents.

Mr. Lewin, bless his heart, let me have the melons for the super-wholesale price of a dime per melon.

I remember having to make four trips down to the highway to lug the huge melons down to my stand. My first day in business I stood all day in the Florida sun, holding my "Watermelons 25 Cents" sign, and didn't sell a single melon. Boy, was I discouraged, especially when I had to haul the melons one at a time back up the hill to Mr. Lewin's garage.

That night, though, I had a revelation: people weren't buying because they couldn't see the immediate benefit of biting into a juicy, crisp slice of watermelon!

Inspiration: what if I sliced the melons into eight pieces and sold the slices for a nickel apiece?

The next day I tried my new approach and my melon business went wild. Hot motorists responded gratefully to the sight of a juicy slice of watermelon being held aloft. Dads and Moms would practically jump from their cars to get slices for their screaming backseat passengers. I sold my thirty-two pieces in about an hour and went back up the hill many times for more melons. I had the weather on my side, too.

The day was excruciatingly hot, just perfect for watermelon sales. When I closed down for the day, I had $3.75 worth of nickels, which I carried home in a bag and carefully spread out on the floor to count.

Nowadays $3.75 will barely get you a medium cappuccino, but in 1955 it seemed like a small fortune. Even though I've had a lot of success since then with my entrepreneurial activities, I can tell you that nothing has ever quite equaled the pure joy of seeing all those nickels spread out on the floor. There was also a satisfaction that day that went far beyond the financial. It was seeing the delight on the faces of all those people as they bit into a cool, sweet watermelon on a hot summer day! It's one thing to give customers what they want, but to see them devour it on the spot is sweet satisfaction indeed. When I went back to school that year, I'd put close to $50 in my savings account.

WHAT I LEARNED

I think those early ventures still guide my thinking. They taught me to focus on what I now think of as Priority No. 1: creating things that make people's lives better. I also do my best to create things that make their faces light up, just like biting into a watermelon on a hot day. By focusing on those qualities, I wake up each day knowing I'm going to spend my time creating value and delight. I've lived in that state of consciousness for decades now. It's what I love, and what I wish for you. The best job of all is doing something that doesn't feel like a job at all.

Acknowledgments

I'm deeply grateful to my beloved mate of the past three decades, Kathlyn Hendricks, for being with me in every exploration that inspired this book. With every passing year, I grow more in awe of the loving-kindness and astute brilliance she radiates. Living in the field of her love is the greatest honor and privilege any person could want. As I say to her nearly every day, "You make me feel like the luckiest man on earth." People of the present and future, I say to you: Study this woman. She is the real deal.

I thank the members of my creative, quirky, and loving family. Amanda, Chris and Helen, Elsie and Imogen; you are on my mind and in my heart every day. I also bow to the memory of my mother, Norma Hendricks; my grandparents Rebecca Delle Garrett Canaday and Elmer Ray Canaday; and my aunts Lyndelle, Catherine, and Audrey.

I'm very grateful to have a literary agent, Bonnie Solow, who is much more than a major professional asset to my life.

She's a treasured friend and confidante, dearly loved by both Kathlyn and myself. I'm also blessed with a staff, led by the indomitable Monika Krajewska, who make it possible for me to accomplish a great deal more than I could ever do on my own. My gratitude to you all is boundless.